Th Wealthy Author

The Wealthy Author

The Fast Profit Method For Writing, Publishing & Selling Your Non-Fiction Book

Joe Gregory

Debbie Jenkins

First Published In Great Britain 2009
by Publishing Academy
www.publishingacademy.com

To experts with muddy boots.
You write the best books.

Contents

Praise

"This is a book every author, at whatever stage of their career, needs to read. It has a wealth of information for every step of the process from coming up with ideas and market research though how to write and finally to the all important how to sell, get paid and become wealthy. One element that completely blew me away was the matrix on page 44, demonstrating demographic niches for a book topic. Within a minute of seeing this page I had 55 new ideas for selling my existing book and more new book ideas than I can count. That page alone was worth more than the price of book but there is so much more usable information than this. The best thing for me about this book is not just the information but how it is presented. It is witty, conversational and easy to read with lots of checklists, charts and graphs. It is a very powerful book that I can see me coming back to time and time again as I climb the publishing ladder to become a wealthy author."

Rintu Basu, author, Persuasion Skills Black Book, www.thenlpcompany.com

"The Wealthy Author is a must read for people who want to not only get published, but sell their existing books too! It is jam packed with actual insider secrets for achieving success in this industry and the information inside is worth much more in both financial and time saving terms than the cover price. I like how the book is written in a very friendly and accessible style with no 'pomp'. It is down to earth and gives you the principles of creating and selling information products online which is a skill-set that you can use time and again. Traditional mainstream publishers will be quaking in their boots when their industry secrets are revealed for just £15. Avoid the common beginners mistakes and fast forward your success as a wealthy author with this un-missable book!"

Nadine Hill, author, The Virtual Assistant Handbook, proprietor, The Dream PA, www.thedreampa.co.uk

"The Wealthy Author is essential reading for authors who want to enjoy real success with their books. It provides a comprehensive start-to-finish guide that every author or aspiring author should read. This book tells the truth, cuts through the crap and will prevent you from making some big mistakes. If you want to be a successful author then you need to read this book."

Simon Hazeldine, speaker and author of Bare Knuckle Selling, Bare Knuckle Negotiating, Bare Knuckle Customer Service and The Inner Winner, www.simonhazeldine.com

"The first secret to being a wealthy author must be to have a great title - and once again Joe and Debs show from the outset that they know and do what they teach! The Wealthy Author is an exciting and invaluable resource for anyone wanting to turn their insights, knowledge and experience into a substantial stream of income."

Dr Andrew Bass, Director, Bass Clusker, www.bassclusker.com

"Joe's one of the nicest guys I know, but that's nothing without talent and he has plenty of that... he's a great marketer and an ace copywriter... If you're into self-publishing, Joe's your guy – he'll put you out there and really work to sell your product."

Peta Heskell, author, Flirt Coach, attractionacademy.com

"Debs and her team are always reliable and certainly know their stuff. She has been a pleasure to work and communicate with and I would recommend her to anyone... she also is expert, creative and has high integrity."

Jo Parfitt, prolific author, writer's coach, www.joparfitt.com

"When I was a manager in the music industry, a book came along called 'This Business of Artist Management' which turned my working world upside down. In my opinion, 'The Wealthy Author' is set to do just that for the publishing industry while shaking many people's long held beliefs about what being an author means. I'm absolutely amazed at the wealth of information in this book, the way it's laid out so logically, and I'm sure it will become an industry bible immediately. I will be keeping my copy to refer to again and again."

Nicola Cairncross, wealth coach, speaker and author of The Money Gym, www.themoneygym.com

Acknowledgements

Once you get 'good' at a thing it's easy to forget who helped you on your way. With that in mind we'd like to bring your attention to the following publishing heroes (all wealthy authors in their own right) for being a page ahead of the rest and generously sharing what they know. Thanks to: Aaron Shepard, Felix Denis, John Kremer, Vernon Coleman, Dan Poynter, Peter Bowerman, Seth Godin, Dan Kennedy, Tim Ferris, Larry Winget, Suzan St Maur, Geoff Burch, Robert Craven, Jo Parfitt and Stuart Goldsmith. We owe you far more than the cover price of your books!

We'd also like to thank all of our authors who took a chance on a small independent publisher and who take our ongoing harassment (we like to think of it as encouragement) with good humour. There are way too many of you to mention by name but you're the reason we still jump out of bed each morning!

Particular thanks go to Nadine Hill - for your eagle eyes and action mindset, Rintu Basu – for your resourcefulness and creativity, Nicola Cairncross – for your unyielding support and loyalty and Simon Hazeldine – for your fearless spirit and walking the talk.

Finally, I'd like to thank all of the con-artists and blaggers trying to take advantage of authors for making us angry enough to set up The Publishing Academy and write this book! We wouldn't have done it without you.

Why Should You Even Listen To Us?

"The more you think you already know – the less you can learn."

www.leanmarketing.co.uk

As I sat down to write this introduction I asked myself the following question.

Why should you even listen to us?

We've only been in the publishing game for six years and, when you consider how long the printing press has been around, that's not too long.

We don't have any official publishing-related qualifications and we've never worked for a big publisher – not even as tea-makers. In fact, neither of us has even been *published* by a big publisher (this was through choice rather than necessity – but we'll get to that later). Plus, if you were to compare our income with someone like JK Rowling's – well it's not quite as much!

Yet, despite all this, we're making a great living from books. We live pretty much where we want to live (which, so far, has included the Norfolk coast and Spain). We do pretty much whatever we want with our time. We know that if we took a year off (as I did when I was ill last year) that the money would still keep coming in. Oh, and we love everything about our jobs – including the people we work with!

And that, for me, is the definition of being a wealthy author.

It's not necessarily about the value of your bank balance (though we'll share plenty of tips for increasing that) but about the value you get for your time!

If you're not quite following me yet then how does this sound?

- ✓ As a wealthy author you'll be able to quit your day job and do whatever you like with your time – which could include writing, travelling, reading, scuba diving, sailing or simply goofing off for a while.

- ✓ Once you've put the effort in up front (this isn't a get rich quick approach) you'll be able to sit back and coast for many years to come as your book continues to generate all the money you need to enjoy an enviable lifestyle.

- ✓ As a wealthy author you'll be able to live and work pretty much anywhere with an internet connection and you won't even have to lump any books around if you don't want to.

- ✓ You'll have other people, we're talking huge organisations here, working around the clock to sell, promote and deliver your books while you do whatever you like.

- ✓ Your time will truly be your own, to spend as you wish! And that – in my book – is priceless! After all, you can always get more money but time runs out for all of us eventually!

Our goal for this book is simple:

To share all the things we've learned over the years (from our successes and failures) about making money from non-fiction books. Our goal is to enable you to free up your time and benefit from a virtually hands-free income from your book or books. All the checklists and tools we share have been created based on hard-won experience (both our own and the many prolific authors we've worked with).

So, follow our advice and I guarantee you'll be able to get where we are now with far less effort and in a far shorter time-frame!

Sound good? Great! Let's get started... But first let me answer my first question. Here's why you should listen to us:

- ✓ We devised and delivered a simple launch plan (which has been much copied since) for one of our authors that sold over £30,000 of books within 24 hours.

- ✓ We have written, published and actively marketed over 70 non-fiction books. Not all of them have been totally successful – but what we've learned from the failures will help you just as much as what we learned from our successes.

✓ We're the creators of the acclaimed Lean Marketing™ system which focuses on high-impact-low-cost marketing tactics that work. Ensuring you get a lot more 'coming in' from your marketing than you have 'going out' is key if you want to be a wealthy author!

✓ We're authors too (we've co-written more than 11 books on low-cost-high-impact marketing) and sold 6,000 copies of our first self-published book within two and a half years. This was before Print On Demand (POD) and without any major distribution, a proper Amazon listing or a single book in a bricks and mortar bookshop. The full case study is included later.

✓ In the last 6 years we've published more than 70 books, created 9 best-sellers and made a very nice living working far fewer hours than we did when we were full-time marketing consultants. And we're willing to share how you can do it too!

So, for my part I plan to provide you with all the direction and motivation you need to make a full-time (and life-time) income as a non-fiction author while doing and spending as little as possible. For simplicity, I'll be your official guide throughout this book, but many of the tools and concepts I share were created by the two of us, so if I wasn't telling you this stuff Debs certainly would be!

Here's to your success as an author! May your future be full of free time, plenty of cash and the fame and happiness you deserve!

Joe Gregory
Moratalla, Spain, August 2009

Is This Book For You?

"Success Secret: Strive to create more value than you consume."

Debbie Jenkins, www.leanmarketing.co.uk

This is a 'How To' book for the authors of *useful* non-fiction books.

Why do I make the distinction 'useful'? Why not *all* non-fiction? Well, because I want to differentiate between books where the reader learns something that they can use, gets answers to a previously unsolvable problem, experiences a life-changing new world view or is able to learn a new skill that will help in life, from books where the reader gets entertainment only.

Biographies, even inspirational ones, don't fall into the 'useful' category because they're designed to get an emotional response rather than to inform. They're entertainment at best and, at worst, they're ego-tainment designed to cash-in on some celebrity's short-lived fame.

Although I'm sure much of this book will be useful to fiction writers and entertainment focused non-fiction authors too, it wasn't written for you. So, if you are planning on using the stuff in this book to peddle your life story, get your poetry read by the masses (which may only happen after you've died of starvation) or write the next *Harry Potter* then you've been warned!

Who Should Read This Book?

✓ If you are seriously ready to start writing your first non-fiction book but have little or no idea how to start then this book, in particular Step 1 and 2, is for you.

✓ If you have a book in print right now and it's not selling as well as you'd like then this book, in particular Step 5, is for you.

✓ Whether you've already self-published your book or landed a contract with a 'proper' publisher this book is for you.

✓ If you firmly believe that the success of your book is in your own hands and down to the actions you take rather than the wishes you make, then this book is for you.

✓ If your book has been in print for a while but just isn't selling, then this book is for you.

✓ If you're a successful (or prolific) author but are frustrated that you still need a day job to make ends meet then this book is for you.

✓ If you're in the early stages of devising your book or need help writing a book that's likely to sell well, then this book is for you.

Who Shouldn't Read This Book?

✗ If you think a book should just do well because it's 'good' and marketing is no task for a 'proper' author, then I'm not interested in trying to change your mind. This book could certainly help you but I'm not going to twist your arm!

✗ If you're hoping for somebody else (publisher, publicist, bookshops) to do all the work to promote your book for you, then this book will just get on your nerves because I will keep reminding you that it's *your* job to sell your book!

✗ If you just saw the 'wealthy' bit of the title and think making money as an author is going to be easy then think again! This book will definitely help you, but you might not like the amount of work you're going to have to put in up front.

✗ If you want yet more theory but are not willing to follow this up with action, then this book will give you lots of cool tools, approaches and tips, but it will not help you become a wealthy author. You need to take consistent and considered action for that to happen!

How To Use This Book

You can dip into the book using the contents page to find tips and tools to help with your current challenges or you can choose the step you're at now (based on the Publishing Ladder of Success – introduced shortly) and go straight to that Step in the book.

However, for the full effect I recommend that you work through the entire book. Even if you have a book in print and are only really interested in getting some tips and selling more copies, I'd suggest you review *that* book using the lists and tools we share before going any further.

A warning though: finding that your book has a major flaw (say with the title or the idea itself) can be a painful experience. It's how you respond to this experience that will set your future direction. Here are your choices:

- ✘ You can deny the obvious fact that you didn't have this useful book when you first started and have made a fundamental error. And then compound that original error by continuing to work hard at the promotion (attempting to force your book to be a success).

- ✓ You can learn from this realisation, put the wasted time and effort behind you and go back to the drawing board (or Word Processor) to make your next book into a winner.

The second option is often quicker and easier but I know it's painful to think back on all the hard work you put in to get where you are now! So here's a bit of wisdom...

"No matter how far you've walked down the wrong road – turn back!"

My top tip is that you skim read the whole book first - it's been kept intentionally short and snappy because it's an action book so it won't take that long – and then either read it in full or find the bits that stand out!

What You're Going To Get From Reading This Book

How To Come Up With Great Book Ideas

Without question a great book idea is the starting point for all wealthy authors. But a good idea alone won't get you very far. By the time you've finished Step 1 of this book you should be able to answer 'yes' to the following ...

- ✓ Do you know if your book idea is really that good?
- ✓ Are you able to easily come up with great ideas whenever you like?
- ✓ Can you sum your book up well with a single sentence?
- ✓ Does your book have a killer title?
- ✓ Do you know how your book is positioned?

How To Find A Market Hungry for Your Book

It only takes one person to believe an idea is great. But, if you only sell *one book* to that *one person* then you're unlikely to become very wealthy! Once you're finished with Step 2 of this book you'll be able to say 'yes' to the following ...

- ✓ Are you confident your great idea has any kind of a commercial future?
- ✓ Do you know how to rapidly test the market and build a list of prospects before writing your book?
- ✓ Can you easily give great reasons why prospective readers should buy your book instead of taking *any* other action?
- ✓ Will your book appeal to 'hungry fanatics' and do you even know how to find them?
- ✓ Can you really say who your book is for without resorting to 'anyone and everyone'?

How To Write Your Book Quickly & Easily

Once you've got a great idea and you know there's a market then it's time to get writing. Once you've sailed through Step 3 you'll be able to shout 'yes' to the following questions...

- ✓ Have you immunised yourself against writer's block?
- ✓ Can you rapidly and easily map out your book before writing a single word?
- ✓ Have you got a useful chapter-by-chapter framework to help your book write itself?
- ✓ Do you know the essential elements you need in your non-fiction book?
- ✓ Would you be able to write a book in a week if you had to?

How To Get Your Book Published

Making the right decision here is crucial. Even if you think your goal is to get a contract from a mainstream publisher or that self-publishing is a last resort for frustrated authors tired of rejection, you need to know your options. Once you've compared the different ways to get your book in print by reading Step 4 you'll be able to say 'yes' to the following...

- ✓ Do you know how to pitch your book idea so that it beats off 99% of the other books?
- ✓ Can you easily spot and avoid the scams, tricks and lies employed by unscrupulous vanity publishers and agents out to steal your money and dreams?
- ✓ If you decide to self-publish do you know how to get your ISBN, barcode and other essential elements of a properly published book?
- ✓ Do you understand the different publishing models well enough to work out which one is the right choice for you?
- ✓ Are you able to maximise profit from your intellectual property by choosing the right publishing approach?

How To Sell Loads of Books & Raise Your Profile

Here's the really important bit. Everything up to this point is academic if you don't actually sell books. The good news is that once you've read Step 5 you'll be able to nod a confident 'yes' to the following...

✓ Do you know why 80% of the 'book publicity activity' authors and publishers spend time and money on is futile?

✓ Are you convinced that marketing is absolutely your responsibility and that you shouldn't leave this most important job to your publisher or publicist?

✓ Do you know hundreds of different things you *could* do to sell more copies of your book but why you only need to focus on doing a *few* of them to succeed?

✓ Can you spot the difference between 'vanity' and 'sanity' marketing activities and use the latter to increase sales while winning back free time by eradicating the former?

✓ Are you confident that you'll be able to promote your book better than anyone else – even if you previously knew absolutely nothing about marketing?

How To Turn One Book Into A Lifetime Income

Selling loads of books is a great start but if you leave it there then you'll always be looking for the next big pay day. In Step 6 you'll learn how to set things up so that you can easily and smugly answer 'yes' to the following...

✓ Do your book sales turn into higher and higher revenues as your readers gladly and eagerly pay more money to get more of your knowledge?

✓ Are you able to command much higher fees as a consultant, speaker, coach or expert than your non-published rivals?

✓ Do you have the mechanisms in place to turn a single book into an impressive full-time income that works pretty-much on autopilot?

- ✓ Will the money from your book-based business continue to pour in – even if you decide not to work another day in your life?
- ✓ Can you see how to experience time freedom (do what you like), physical freedom (from wherever you like) and financial freedom (without worrying about money) by setting things up right from the start?

Essential Principles All Wealthy Authors Understand & Apply

*"If you're tired of coming up against a
brick wall then build a ladder."*

Joe Gregory, www.leanmarketing.co.uk

Where Are You On The Publishing Ladder of Success?

The business of writing and selling books is a lot like a ladder. If you're currently on the ground and you want to get higher then you need to take certain steps along the way. Attempting to skip a step on the way up can be dangerous and, as you get higher, the consequences of failure are greater too. So if you intend to succeed as an author then you need to pay attention and take things carefully.

The 6 Steps To Becoming A Wealthy Author

1. **Creativity:** Coming up with good book ideas.

2. **Viability:** Identifying and finding a market for your book.

3. **Productivity:** Writing the book quickly and easily.

4. **Tangibility:** Getting your book in print – whether you plan to land a publisher or self-publish.

5. **Publicity:** Selling loads of books – including everything from raising your profile, getting reviews and getting good distribution.

6. **Longevity:** Cashing in on your position as an author – using your newfound authority to get paid bigger fees and turning one book (or more) into a full time income that can pay you for the rest of your life.

Steps 1, 2 and 3 are essentially all part of the creative phase. Although you're not likely to stay here too long getting these steps wrong will make the rest of the game of becoming a wealthy author much more difficult.

Step 4 – getting your book in print – is often the first stumbling block for many would-be authors. But, as you'll soon discover, there is no longer any real barrier to getting your book in print.

Step 5 – selling loads of books – is the second stumbling block. The good news is that failure at this point is almost always down to one of two things: either the author doesn't have a clue how to sell their book (which will be fixed when you finish Step 5) or the author didn't take responsibility for selling their book (which, by the fact you're reading this now, doesn't include you). However, selling loads of books isn't going to make you rich by itself. Step 6 – cashing in – is the often-missing and unknown step where the real wealth lies.

MAKE MONEY

TURN ONE BOOK INTO WEALTH
6. LONGEVITY

SELL LOADS OF BOOKS
5. PUBLICITY

GET YOUR BOOK PUBLISHED
4. TANGIBILITY

GET YOUR BOOK WRITTEN
3. PRODUCTIVITY

COST MONEY

FIND A MARKET FOR YOUR BOOK
2. VIABILITY

COME UP WITH IDEAS EASILY
1. CREATIVITY

The bottom of this ladder (at least the first 3 steps and often the 4th) costs you money so you really don't want to linger on the creation phase. You may think you're only spending time during the writing phase but the fact is this. If you *weren't* writing a book you could be spending that same time earning money doing a 'proper' job, being paid by clients or selling your existing book. This is an 'opportunity cost' because when you're spending time creating your next masterpiece you'll be forfeiting the opportunity to earn money now.

As I've already said, the top of the ladder is where the real wealth is, which is why our aim is to get you there as quickly as possible.

This book has been devised to help you move easily and quickly from the first step to the last... but where are you now?

Stuck With Your Head In Your Ass-ets: Steps 1 to 3

If you're hanging around at the bottom of the ladder (steps 1 to 3) then your book project will be costing you time, energy and money but will not bring in a single penny of income.

Too many people stay here for far too long, but the reality is that if you want to be a wealthy author you can't afford to. Doing loads of competitor and market research, or obsessing over your pitch, or taking too long to get the book written will all lead to more up-front cost for you and a bigger up-front investment which eats into your eventual profit!

Stuck With A Book But No Publisher: Step 4

If your book project stalls here then you could have real trouble. Not only have you invested time, energy and possibly money up front, but if you fail to get your big idea into the hands of prospective buyers then there is zero chance that your hard work is ever going to pay off! At this stage your options are...

1. **Land a deal with a mainstream publisher.** If you're after kudos over profits or the thought of sorting out ISBNs, book cover designs, editing, typesetting and distribution yourself scares you (though you'll find most of this stuff is easy once you know how) – then this is the way to go. While you don't get to keep 100% of the profit (most mainstream publishers are seen as generous if they give you 7%) you aren't taking a whole lot of the up-front risk either. If you have dreams of a nice fat advance then dream on; many publishers are doing away with this model and unless you're already a celebrity (or big name author) you're not very likely to get one.

2. **Self-publish.** This is my preferred approach, especially for non-fiction as you get to keep control and keep 100% of the profit. Of course you also take 100% of the risk too and there's a lot of work to do in the early stages before you'll see a penny back. With more and more Print on Demand (POD) companies (I'm talking printers and not vanity publishers) entering the market, self-publishing is getting easier! As you'll see, the work really begins when the book is in print. You'll need to be ready for some hard work and a steep learning curve – but that's why you're reading this book – right?

3. **Pay to publish.** Whether they call themselves collaborative publishers, subsidy publishers or co-operative publishers the simple fact is that they're really just vanity publishers. As if the cost of getting this far isn't great enough, many of these companies charge more than they're worth up-front and then make an obscene profit by selling your own books to you. No matter what they say you'll still have to market the hell out of your book *and* you'll have a bigger hill to climb to break even. This really isn't an option for a wealthy author and I'll show you precisely why later in this book.

Stuck With A Book That's Not Selling: Step 5

Sadly, this is where most authors end up stuck. You have a great book, you've invested loads of time, energy and possibly money (if not yours then your publishers) and it's out there but it's just not selling.

To be honest some books are doomed to stay here (though you won't have this problem once you've read this book) because the author (or publisher) didn't bother to check there was a market! It doesn't matter how good a book is, if a market doesn't exist for it then you ain't gonna sell it!

But what if there is a huge market? What if the content in your book really answers that market's need? What if it's not selling then? This will usually be a result of one (or all) of the following...

1. **The author is not doing enough active promotion**. As someone who's been on both sides of the fence I'm sincere when I say that promoting your book is 100% the author's responsibility. Blaming your publisher for not promoting your book or complaining about your position on the book shelf or hoping your book will sell because it's so much better than the others is stupid! It's your book. It's your profile. It's *your* responsibility to get it selling. If you don't know how then you will when you've finished reading this book! But never forget, make no excuses, all successful authors with few exceptions got there by taking responsibility for their promotion and taking consistent action to get their book selling. If they say they didn't then they were either very lucky or they're lying!

2. **The book's packaging is awful**. Problems include a poor book cover (the cover is the most important selling device you have so don't leave it to amateurs), a poor book blurb (if your book doesn't tell readers what's in it for them but instead bores them to tears then your book will struggle), incorrect pricing (it doesn't have to be cheap but it does need to fit your market's expectations and budget) and rubbish or non-existent endorsements (social proof sells, so get some!) Unfortunately most self-publishers cut corners on packaging when it's a major key to success. We'll share plenty of tips for reviewing your book's packaging and principles for getting it right but, for the implementation, we suggest you use experts (either by going with a proper publisher or paying).

3. **The distribution is wrong.** If your book is not featured where people go to buy books then it's going to be hard to sell them. Directly selling your own book, unless you've got a very high-value product and you are an expert direct marketer, is stupid! We closed down our own online bookshop because we quickly realised that it wasn't worth competing with Amazon and Barnes & Noble for sales when we could instead focus on driving all our sales through to them. People trust them. They're a better book retailer than us. They employ loads of people to pack orders, send books and handle returns. They have their own merchant accounts. Sure, we could keep extra profit by selling direct, but we'd also need to employ full time staff to check orders and dispatch books if we wanted to provide a good service. It's simply not worth it. I'd personally focus on the 'killer apps' for book sales – Amazon, Waterstones, Barnes & Noble – first and then look at offline bookshops second.

Stuck With Sales But No (or Low) Income: Step 6

Most authors never get past this point. Selling loads of books is one thing but it's not the real secret of getting rich. If you've controlled costs, negotiated a decent royalty (anything less than 10% is going to be small change unless you're really lucky) and done the promotion right you'll be making an income from your book but it's probably not quite as much as you'd like.

So what do you do?

You could write and publish another ten or more books until the combined income from *all* of them is enough to make you wealthy and happy. That's one strategy (and it's a fine strategy) employed by many rich and successful publishers. But I won't lie. Each time you step on 'the ladder' you're taking a risk with your time, energy and money, and at some level, you'll be playing a numbers game; some books will do well, others will be fantastic flops! In most cases your successes will end up funding your failures, so you'll have worked much harder for only a little more income.

We have another approach however. If you actually start your book project with this sixth step – long term wealth – in mind then you can construct every aspect of your book (and it's marketing) to lead to big rewards for you as it becomes more popular. When you know this secret you'll realise that the real money in books isn't in books at all… but you'll have to wait until the end of the book to find out more!

The Hard Truths About Making Money As An Author

Writing The Book is The Easy Part

That's right! It's just one of six essential steps to becoming a wealthy author and it's given far too much attention. I don't say this to take anything away from the skill of a good writer but think about it…

Plenty of badly written books, by snake oil merchants peddling happy-clappy, feel-good, 'the-universe-will-provide' nonsense have made the bestseller lists. I've read books that were absolutely awful that sell by the truck-full. I've also read brilliantly written books that most people have never heard of.

So what does this prove? It proves that, at least for the purpose of making money from books, the writing doesn't really matter very much at all. I'm not telling you this because I think it's a *good* thing but it is a *true* thing.

Don't join the hordes of idealistic, but often starving, authors who believe:

"If I write something that's good enough then they will come [and buy it]!"

In an ideal world maybe! But, I'm here to tell you that the *real* world plays by different rules. I don't want you to starve for your art. I want you to get paid, and get paid well, for your effort. That means realising that the writing part is really just a *small* portion of the success equation and you should get it done as quickly and cost-effectively as possible.

If You Don't Know The Subject Then Don't Write A Book On It

I hope you wouldn't even be thinking of writing a non-fiction book unless you knew something other people needed to know. Unless you were an expert with great information to pass on. Unless you had an important message that needed spreading.

Too often you get 'professional' writers who base their book idea on what might sell well or what their publisher wants. They figure that they can research the important stuff and their amazing writing ability will ensure the book is a great success.

But here's the problem. If you do the promotion right then you're going to be 'fronting' your book the whole way. It's really just an extension of what you know. So you're going to need credibility, passion, knowledge or a good story to pull it off. There's plenty of poor non-fiction out there so don't add to it!

In essence, and I'm about to rant here, if you're reading this book because you think writing a book is an easy way to make loads of money and you think you can just bodge some research together, put a nice cover on it and make a fortune then you need to think again! And then, after you've thought again, if you're still thinking that you don't need to be an expert on, or have a genuine passion for your subject in order to write a book may I suggest... [Deb's note: I removed Joe's suggestion because it wasn't nice!]

There Are Easier & Safer Ways To Make Lots of Money

Beware anyone who tells you that writing a book is an easy way to get rich. It's not! Writing and publishing a book is massively front- loaded with risk. You have to invest lots of time and resources up front before you can make it pay. The book isn't going to sell itself. There are many barriers to success. Many authors never even get beyond their advance in sales revenue. Being an author really is not for everyone, which is a good thing!

Because, once you've overcome the obstacles and made it work, you'll find you're in a great position. You'll be earning royalties whether you work or not. You'll have other people doing all the donkey-work. You'll have invested *one* chunk of time just *one time* for multiple rewards. You'll be leaving a legacy and impacting far more lives than you could in any other way.

An easy (or fool-proof) way to make money? No way. This book will help you to succeed quickly but if you're risk averse then get a regular job! It's safer.

First-Time Authors Are Seen As An Easy Target By Scammers

From vanity presses (selling you over-priced publishing services and taking the lion's share of the profit) to unscrupulous publishers expecting you to enter their competition (and pay an entrance fee) in order to win a publishing contract, you'll find plenty of people looking to take your money off you and provide nothing but broken dreams in return.

Here are some basic rules to keep you safe:

- ✓ If they (agent/publisher) ask you to pay them a fee in order to review your synopsis or proposal then they're not to be trusted.
- ✓ If they ask you to pay to enter a competition to potentially win a publishing contract then they're not to be trusted.
- ✓ If they want to feature you in a compilation but expect you to commit to buying a quantity of books in order to be featured then they're not to be trusted.
- ✓ If they ask you for any money in order to get your book (or writing) published (unless they are a printer) then they're not to be trusted.
- ✓ A flashy logo, professional looking website, testimonials from other 'authors' or even big name endorsements are no guarantee of their trustworthiness. So don't get carried away with their hype.

Why Wealthy Authors Are Also Lazy Authors

"Laziness is a virtue. Make it your daily mission to stop doing anything that doesn't bring a reward."

Joe Gregory, www.leanmarketing.co.uk

The working title for this book was 'The Lazy Author' I actually think it's more accurate than the title we went with (as our goal for you is that you can get paid again and again while sitting on your backside) but there's too much stigma attached to the word 'lazy' and so it didn't make for the most unambiguous or aspirational title.

But to be a 'Lazy Author' is both a *means* and an *end...*

It's a means because, by getting into the lazy mindset, you'll always be striving to find the easiest, quickest and least time-consuming ways to come up with, write and sell as many books as possible.

If you're usually mega-busy and believe that nothing gets done without hard work then I want you to try the lazy mindset on for the duration of this book. You'll be surprised at the results that can be achieved when you do only the *right* things instead of *every* thing.

'Lazy' is also an end because I'm sure you'd like to spend your time doing *anything* but work. And when your book (or books) are bringing in all the money you need then you can then spend your time exactly how you wish. This could be lazing half the year sipping cocktails while lying in a hammock on an exotic island, travelling the world, learning something new or fulfilling whatever personal dreams you have right now.

Once you get your books selling using the systems outlined in *The Wealthy Author* they'll continue to sell even if you never lift a finger to promote them ever again. Allowing you true laziness because you did the right things up front!

Sure, laziness has had a pretty bad press over the years but I want you to embrace it. If you're lazy and *unsuccessful* then you may have a problem but if you're lazy and *very successful* then the only people criticising you will be doing it out of envy.

Being lazy is a useful, honourable and admirable trait. I want you to be clear on this fact because you will have been conditioned your whole life to believe the exact opposite. So the only way to find the proof is to try it out.

Wanting to do as little as possible, for the biggest reward, is to be admired. The natural human drive to do less and get more has been responsible for much of humankind's progress from knuckle-dragging apes to the mobile, connected and (mostly) civilised people we are today.

We've been conditioned by successive 'authorities' to think that hard work is the means to success, or even our duty, but it's not. It's a trick to ensure our 'leaders' have an obedient and productive workforce so they can get fat off our labour! This is known as the 'Pharaoh Principle' and I'm going to show you how to turn the tables and make it work *for* you instead of against you later in the book.

Think about it. If hard work really translated to more success then bricklayers, cleaners and nurses would be being paid a hell of a lot more. And professional sports stars wouldn't be earning the equivalent of a surgeon's yearly salary every week. Most of the people who do the hardest work – the work that requires the most physical exertion, has the poorest working conditions and provides the least kudos – are paid the least in our society. It's not necessarily fair but it *is* true.

Modern economics doesn't care about inputs (effort), it pays based on outputs (results) and the amount people are willing to pay for those outputs. So, if you don't like the term lazy at least think in terms of 'maximising output while minimising input'. You can see it as being 'productively lazy', which means always:

- ✓ Looking for the easiest way to achieve a favourable result.
- ✓ Seeking ways to reduce the number of steps needed to get a desired outcome.
- ✓ Systemising everything you do, from writing your book, to writing your proposals, to writing your press releases.
- ✓ Finding things/activities that work and repeating them.
- ✓ Finding things that don't work and eliminating them.

Occam's Razor

William Occam was a mediaeval philosopher credited with imparting the following wisdom...

> *"Pluralitas non est ponenda sine necessitas."*
> *(Plurality should not be posited without necessity.)*

Now this sounds a little bit too pompous and academic for my liking so here's my simplification...

> *"If you have to choose between two actions*
> *that are both likely to create the same*
> *outcome then choose the simpler one."*

Occam, probably the first truly lazy author of modern times also said...

> *"It is vain to do with more what*
> *can be done with less."*

Now, if you had a problem with being lazy then how does being vain grab you?

The Vital Few and Trivial Many (80/20 Principle)

We'll be revisiting this rule often, especially when it comes to your marketing, but here are the basics...

In 1906 Italian economist Vilfredo Pareto created a mathematical formula to describe the unequal distribution of wealth in his country, observing that twenty percent of the people owned eighty percent of the wealth.

Later, after Pareto had created his formula, many others observed similar phenomena in their fields of expertise.

Quality Management pioneer, Dr. Joseph Juran recognised that there was, in fact, a universal principle which he called the 'vital few and trivial many'.

As a result of similarities between the original observation by Pareto 30 odd years earlier, Dr. Juran's observation of the 'vital few and trivial many' became known as Pareto's Principle or the 80/20 Rule.

Juran's (or Pareto's) Principle can be simply stated as...

"20 percent of your effort is typically responsible for 80 percent of your results"

This rule is good news because it means you can do less work and get a good way (if not all the way) to achieving your goals. I told you you'd get more success by doing less didn't I?

So, if you have a list of 100 things you were planning on doing I'm here to tell you that just doing 20 of those things will be responsible for 80% of your wealth from books.

To put it another way you should easily be able to work just one day (8 hours) a week to get 80% of the results you'd have gotten from working 5 days (40 hours) a week.

Of course, it's not quite that simple but it's worth bearing in mind at all times that you're almost certainly doing a hell of a lot of trivial stuff that you'd be better off not doing.

This book will help you to focus on the good stuff and stop doing the rest.

Step 1: Coming Up With A Winning Book Idea

"The first idea you come up with is often the worst. So why is the first idea where most people stop?"

Debbie Jenkins, www.leanmarketing.co.uk

You may be one of those lucky people who are falling over themselves with ideas for books! If you are then congratulations you'll enjoy this bit. You can use the checklists, tools and self-tests to help you to review your ideas and pick the one most likely to pay off! See it as a process of elimination rather than creation!

If, however, you're like most people then you may struggle to come up with new ideas. Or, you may have a good idea but you don't know how to make it truly great. If this is you then you'll love this section of the book. I'll show you ways to generate plenty of new ideas, how to position your idea to be unique, test it to find ways to improve it and even come up with a winning title. But first, let's just talk a little about getting into the right state...

The Creative State

A lot of people get really caught up here, "I'm not feeling creative today!", "I'm just not in the mood!", "All my creativity has slipped from my body and I'm left like a parched and bitter shell of my former self..." Well whatever your (creative) excuse, here's the news: creativity is a process. Creative people are simply better at running this process (whether they do it consciously or not) than their less creative (and slightly more envious) peers.

So, now you know there are steps to follow and creativity is not some magical ability that you have to barter your soul to possess, let's first look at your state.

8 Tips For Getting Into A More Creative State of Mind

1. Get yourself somewhere comfortable and clear from clutter.

2. Clear your mind with whatever works for you. I suggest doing something like listening to or playing music, going for a walk, drawing or painting or having a long bath. If you're into meditation or yoga then use that.

3. Silence your inner critic. You know that voice in your head that edits stuff before it comes out of your mouth? Well it's useful a lot of the time but it can really stifle creativity! So first, accept that it is useful in some contexts (specifically when you don't want to say something stupid) and then just agree with yourself that it's okay to give this critical 'voice' a little break, for say the next 30 minutes.

4. Pose yourself creative questions using words like, "How can I?", "What if?", "What's interesting about?"

5. Dwell on an idea. If you have a skill, a theme or an over-riding feeling about what you want to create then meditate upon it. Simply let it expand to fill your mind and let the connections in your brain start happening.

6. Take a notebook to bed. Just before you enter deep sleep your mind is at its most creative. The problem is that any good ideas you dream up while sleeping are often forgotten by the time you wake up. So, take a notebook to bed and let inspiration strike. If your unconscious knows your intention is to record any good ideas that pop into your head you'll be able to wake up and record them.

7. Remind yourself that creativity is as fundamental to being human as being able to breathe. The very fact that you're here at all required massive amounts of creativity. You solve problems every single day that call for creativity. So, if you've been told you're not creative and you've believed it in the past then it's time to grow out of this old and inaccurate belief.

8. Remember times when you've been at your most creative. Feel what you felt, see what you could see and hear what you heard at the time. Now consciously practice feeling those same feelings in the here and now! That's right, you've already been creative so you can do it again, whenever you want.

4 Surefire Ways To Stifle Creativity

The following tips aren't very useful for being creative, so if you catch yourself doing any of these things then cut it out!

1. Trying to be creative. The very act of 'trying' pre-supposes that you're not 'being' creative. Stop beating yourself up if ideas aren't coming easily and take a break. Then when inspiration strikes again – which it will – be prepared to jump into action.

2. Self editing too early. Be prepared to accept and acknowledge any and every idea that pops into your head whilst generating ideas. Otherwise it's like trying to simultaneously accelerate with one foot while keeping your other foot on the brake pedal.

3. Talking yourself out of being creative. We've already covered this but just to make it clear, all humans are creative, it's what separates us from pretty much all other living species. So stop the negative chatter. Ignore the past and enjoy it.

4. Not having fun. If you're doing it right then the creative process will be a lot of fun. So, if you're feeling angry, frustrated or annoyed whilst doing this then you need to stop and take a break. See it as a game and take yourself lightly instead and you'll find it hard not to have fun while being creative.

The 3 Perceptual Positions for Creativity

Another element to getting into a creative state is to 'act as if' you're somebody else and see things from that perspective (or perceptual position). This is a typical NLP (Neurolinguistic Programming) approach and is very powerful for finding new perspectives on things. For the purpose of creativity this process can be a lot of fun and can really get out of hand (in a good way) if you want it to. Here are the basics.

1. 1st Position – Yourself – as an author or expert (or you could really have fun and be 'yourself' with the imagined creative powers of Walt Disney, Edward de Bono, Einstein, Mozart etc).

2. 2nd Position – Your Audience(s) – prospective readers, reviewers, peers, opponents, competitors etc. Wherever possible try to imagine someone who's real and whose behaviour and mannerisms you know well then caricature this (take things to the extreme).

3. 3rd Position (Meta Position) – Someone who observes both 'You' and 'Your Audience' from another position – although this could be strung out to infinity as you continue to observe the observer observing the observed ad infinitum.

How To Use The Perceptual Positions

1. Come up with ideas from your own (first) position – set yourself a time limit of say 10 minutes for this.

2. Then step into the shoes of your prospective audience (second) and see what new ideas you can generate. Spend another 5-10 minutes for each one.

3. Finally, imagine you are a third party watching yourself and your audience interacting (third) and see what else pops up. Spend another 10 minutes here and review the interaction(s) making any notes.

4. Go back to your first position (as yourself) and come up with any final ideas based on what you've learned.

5. Some people find stepping into these different roles easier if they actually choose three distinct locations to 'step into' - 3 different chairs (or rooms) for instance.

What Would Walt Disney Do? WWWDD

A specific strategic application of perceptual positions can be found in the work of Neurolinguistic Programming pioneer Robert Dilts who, for want of a better description, modelled the strategies of dead geniuses and recorded them in his *Strategies of Genius* book series. This particular use of perceptual positions is based on the creativity of Walt Disney.

Walt Disney developed three distinct modes of thinking:

✓ The Dreamer (unrestrained creativity) – would say:
- o I get excited by new ideas.
- o I'm always looking for better ways to do things.
- o I don't like limitations.

✓ The Realist (practical yet supportive) – would say:
- o I need all the facts to make a decision.
- o I must know everything I can about this.
- o I want to know what's real and what's not.

✓ The Spoiler (pessimistic and contrarian) – would say:
- o I expect perfection.
- o Yes but...
- o I need to know all the risks.

He could adopt any one of these roles at different times and as one employee said, "You never knew which Walt was coming to your meeting."

Using The WWWDD Creative Approach

1. Set a creative outcome or goal you want to achieve.
2. State the outcome in positive terms (ie "I want..." rather than "I *don't* want...")
3. From the *Dreamer* mindset visualise the outcome being successfully achieved and come up with ideas by asking the *Dreamer* questions...
   a. If time, money, knowledge, skill etc. are not a problem what would I do/create/be?
   b. What do I want?
   c. Why do I want it?
   d. What is good (beneficial) about this?
   e. What will the finished thing look or be like?
   f. How else? What else?
4. Then get into the *Realist* mindset and ask the *Realist* questions to improve the original *Dreamer* ideas...
   a. How can we make this idea work?
   b. How can this be achieved practically?

    c. What are the limitations?

    d. What specifically does this involve?

    e. What legal/financial/time implications are there?

    f. What limitations are there?

5. Then get into the *Spoiler* mindset and ask the *Spoiler* questions to check the viability of the improved ideas to uncover problems...

    a. What's wrong with this idea?

    b. What could go wrong with this plan?

    c. How do you know this is a good idea?

    d. What's the worst that could happen if it failed?

    e. What crucial questions need to be answered?

6. Finally, take any problems back to the *Dreamer* and *Realist* positions to come up with further solutions and ideas.

7. Repeat this cycle until the *Spoiler* is no longer able to come up with problems or until you're happy you've achieved the creative output you were seeking.

It's no surprise that Walt Disney's approach fits almost perfectly with...

The 3 Phases of The Creative Process

Often people get stuck with 'being creative' because they're unaware that there is a sequence of steps that, if you try to do them all at once, will result in the flow of new ideas simply freezing up. To help avoid this 'brain freeze' it's worth following these steps.

1. Generating Ideas

1. Any and every idea is fair game here.

2. Don't self edit or criticise - simply record all the ideas you come up with.

3. Put yourself into different perceptual positions (as explained earlier) to come up with more ideas.

4. Use word association, brainstorming, mind mapping (all explained shortly) or any other method of generating and recording ideas that works best for you.
5. I prefer to cut up loads of scraps of waste paper into little squares so I can reorder, remove and group them easily at the review stage.

2. Reviewing Ideas

1. Now is the time to allow your inner critic its say.
2. Typically this will involve a process of elimination.
3. Sort ideas onto a Keep or Kill scale:

KEEP | | | | | | | | KILL

4. Once you've sorted through your ideas I'd suggest using Mind Mapping® (a little more analytical than other generative techniques) to record the outcome of the reviewing stage with room to add more at the improving stage.

3. Improving/Testing Ideas

1. Choose your top 5 ideas and see how you can build on them (this will be easier once you've read the whole of this section).

2. If you've created a Mind Map® then add further depth to it.

3. Refine your ideas until you have a solid selection of good ones.

4. Choose your favourite and add further meat to the bare bones until you've got a theoretical prototype or test case all planned out.

Creative Approaches For Authors

Word Association

1. Choose an overriding theme (you could base this on your prospective target market or your area of expertise) and sum it up in a simple word or phrase.

2. Start writing any words, phrases or ideas that come to mind. This is often better if you have two or more people to bounce ideas off.

3. Keep going and continue to add associations. It's up to you if you continue to associate from the initial word (branching out from a central point) or if you keep moving from one word to the next (to create a stream of consciousness).

4. I recommend using sticky notes (or cut up squares of scrap paper) and sticking them all over a wall or table. Then, once you're done, grab any that jump out at you and see how you can combine these ideas to make new connections.

5. When you've stopped generating ideas (or after say 30 minutes - just in case you don't stop generating ideas) you're ready to review.

Brainstorming

While Mind Mapping® is a great creative tool nothing beats effective brainstorming for pure idea-generating power. In fact, too many people overlook this approach because it's been around for so long but I urge you to use it anyway because it works. Here are some simple rules for getting the best out of brainstorming sessions:

1. It's best to get at least 3 people together – although you could always do this yourself using the perceptual positions method introduced earlier.

2. Pose a central question to be answered, or outcome to achieve, like: "How many ways can an author make money from books?" or "We want at least 30 book title ideas to do with publishing."

3. Choose one 'scribe' or 'facilitator' (it's this person's job to listen carefully and write down what people say).

4. Write down *exactly* what people say – 'Parrot Phrase' don't 'Para Phrase'.

5. Record *every* idea, even if you think it's stupid or a reworded repeat of a previous one.

6. Nobody is allowed to discuss the merits (or not) of ideas going up, they can only *add* ideas. I like to ban the words "but" or "yes but" when doing this.

7. Once all the ideas are recorded you're ready to review.

Mind Mapping® Your Book Ideas

Mind Mapping® was developed by Tony Buzan in the late 1960s and is now used by millions of people around the world for creativity, note taking, planning, studying and improving memory. I personally prefer to use Mind Mapping® to further review and refine my initial brain dump produced from brainstorming because it's a much more cerebral and deliberate technique that requires more time.

"[Mind Mapping] harnesses the full range of cortical skills – word, image, number, logic, rhythm, colour and spatial awareness – in a single, uniquely powerful manner."

Tony Buzan

If you're not already familiar with Mind Mapping® then I'll give you a brief overview here but I strongly urge you to read more on the subject by buying and reading *The Mind Map Book* by Tony and Barry Buzan...

1. Have your page in landscape format (its longest edge running side to side).

2. Choose a central theme, topic or keyword for your creativity session.

3. Draw a picture of your main theme or idea in the centre of the page.

4. Draw your first main branch.

5. Add just one word on this branch, I like to use capital letters.

6. Add sub-branches coming off this main branch.

7. Again add just one word per branch, it will allow more flexibility.

8. Add sub-branches coming off the sub-branches – go 3, 4 or more levels deep.

9. Add as many images as you can next to key themes and ideas as you go, it's best if you draw them for maximum effect.

10. If ideas on distant parts of the map are related then draw dotted lines, arrows or images to connect them up.

Four Mind Mapping® Tips For Authors

1. It doesn't matter if you're a great artist or not the mere process of drawing will activate different parts of your brain that are linked to creativity.

2. Use as many colours as you like, colour enables you to link ideas visually and it also stimulates different brain processes.

3. Your brain quite literally works by association and this process is a really powerful way to mimic the brain's natural ability enabling you to get a lot more of the creative stuff out of your head and onto the page.

4. If it feels relevant number your main branches to put things in order.

Here's an example of a hand-drawn Mind Map® around Love created by Slark at *www.flickr.com/slark* ...

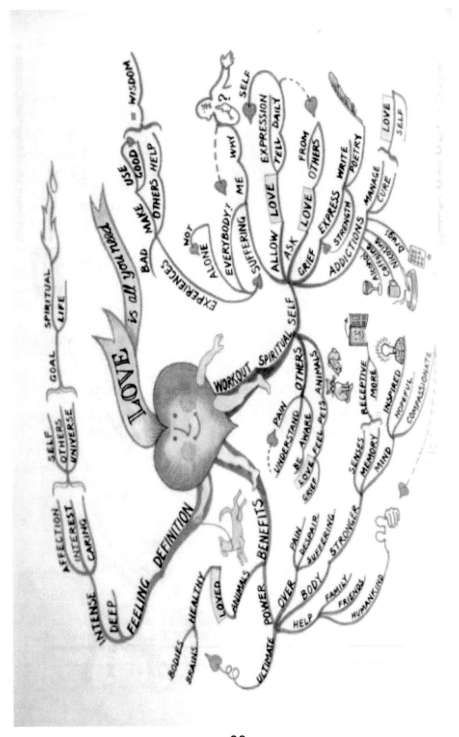

Mind Mapping® Software

iMindMap from *www.imindmap.com/bookshaker* which was created with Tony Buzan himself enables you to quickly and easily produce printable and shareable Mind Maps. This is a commercial package and comes with very powerful features that provide you with beautiful and editable Mind Maps.

However, while not as beautiful, easy-to-use, nor fully featured as iMindMap, you could also use FreeMind (available for free from *http://freemind.sourceforge.net*). It's certainly not as powerful or feature-rich as iMindMap but the price tag (free) is always appealing!

Self Test: Is Your Big Idea A Potential Bestseller?

The big idea is the driving force behind the rest of your book. It's the foundation for everything that follows. Get it right and your book will almost write itself, people will talk about it, the packaging will be strong, the marketing will seem effortless and journalists will love you. Get it wrong and the writing will be tough, people won't notice it, the packaging will be bland, the marketing will seem impossible, journalists will ignore you.

Score your book on the following components as follows: 0 = disagree totally, 1 = agree slightly, 2 = agree totally

My Book...

☐ Makes a big promise that's attractive to readers.

☐ Answers one of life's big questions.

☐ Solves something no other book has solved.

☐ Stands strongly for a particular thing, idea or belief.

☐ Stands strongly against a particular thing, idea or belief.

☐ Fits well within a universally popular interest or trend.

☐ Is considered unique, cool, outrageous, contentious or dangerous.

☐ Fits a niche market with at least 3 associated magazines.

☐ Provides timeless wisdom/principles that won't go out of date.

☐ Provides hard-to-find how-to information on a particular subject.

☐ Is written by a 'go to expert' on the subject.

☐ Is the first or best on a hot new topic or trend.

☐ Makes people say, "You've just got to read this!"

☐ Is packed with sound-bites that people can share and quote easily.

☐ Can be summed up effectively in one sentence.

YOUR SCORE

0-9: Back to the drawing board! This isn't a good idea yet and if you go ahead without trying to improve it then you're going to have to work hard to make it sell. So ask yourself, "How can I make this idea tick more boxes?" If you're not sure keep reading for tips and tools to help you.

10-19: Room for improvement! Your book, with the right promotion, will probably do okay but isn't it worth making the idea better before you go through all the hard work to come? So, ask yourself, "How can I make this idea tick more boxes?" Then keep reading to learn some tricks.

20+: We would publish it! Your book idea is truly a thing of beauty. But the idea is just the first step on a long publishing journey. You'll need to execute the writing, packaging and marketing impeccably to really benefit from your idea's full potential. Talk to us at *www.bookshaker.com/authors* if you need a publisher.

30: You cheated! Some of the components of a winning book idea conflict with others. So, please re-do the test and actually read and think this time! However, if you really *did* score 30 then we'd like to hear your idea and maybe interview you! Tell us at *www.publishingacademy.com/contact*

What's Your Book's Positioning Strategy?

Although positioning is often seen as a marketing task your book's position must be clear right from the outset because it has a profound effect on how the book is written, how it is packaged, how it is marketed and much more.

Now, lots of over-complicated nonsense has been written on positioning – and some people waste a small fortune on it – but it really just boils down to this:

"Stand for something or stand against something. If you stay in the middle you stand for nothing."

Debbie Jenkins, www.leanmarketing.co.uk

Use the following simple scale to determine your book's position. The more extreme the better. If you're in the middle then you'll get lost amongst all the other 'me-too' stuff on your subject.

AGAINST								FOR

We'll look at positioning your book in relation to the competition in Step 2.

A Rigorous Book Positioning Tool That Leaves No Page Unturned

If the above positioning strategy seems too simplistic for you and you'd rather wrestle with your book's positioning in more detail to ensure you've missed nothing out then you'll enjoy using this powerful tool.

There are three main ways we sort data in our minds. They are:

1. Chunking Up (where you'll get all the benefits/problems and reasons why/why not).

2. Chunking Down (where you'll get all the detail of what something is or is not).

3. Chunking Laterally (where you'll get metaphors, analogies and examples of what a thing is like or is unlike).

Now you know the basics of chunking here's how to use it...

1. Get a big sheet of paper.

2. Write a theme, topic, audience, main idea or your subject in the centre (draw it as a picture too if you like).

3. Draw your own matrix copying the image on the next page.

4. Use the questions in the image to help you chunk in all the directions (up, down, lateral) and against (left) and for (right) from the main theme.

5. Ideally write all your ideas on post-it notes so you can easily sort them and move them around to help find your position.

6. Use this information to clearly state...

   o What your book *is not* or does not stand for.
   o What your book *is* or does stand for.
   o What your book *won't* give readers.
   o What your book *will* give readers.
   o What subjects your book won't cover.
   o What subjects your book will cover.
   o Who your book *is not* for.
   o Who your book *is* for.

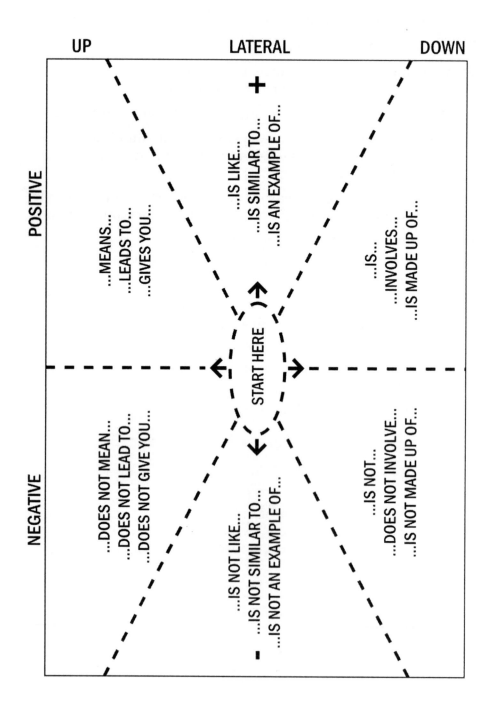

8 Book Title Creation Basics

Your book's title is probably the single most important thing to consider at the initial ideas stage. Sure, some publishers will want to change it, but your title (even when pitching to publishers) says a lot about you, your position and your book's chances. So never underestimate the power of a good title!

1. Don't try to be clever if a more obvious title is stronger.
2. If you do have a clever, witty or one-word main title then be sure your sub-title explains your book's big promise.
3. Your title's number one job is to make people want to open the book.
4. A good title is like a good headline so model newspapers and magazines.
5. Make your title dramatic and use powerful, active and emotive words.
6. Make a big promise or say something shocking or provocative.
7. Ask a leading question to make prospective readers curious.
8. Pose a conundrum that will engage your audience.

17 Words That Add Power To Any Book Title

1. How To
2. Secrets of
3. Stop
4. Start
5. Discover
6. Unleash
7. Change
8. Never
9. Always
10. Unlock
11. Beat
12. Free
13. You, Your
14. Ways To
15. The Key To
16. The Secret To
17. Master

Self Test: Does Your Book Have A Killer Title?

Score your title on the following components as follows:
0 = disagree totally, 1 = agree slightly, 2 = agree totally

My Book's Title...

☐ Makes a big promise.

☐ Poses a question.

☐ Says something contentious, shocking or risky.

☐ Creates curiosity.

☐ Is unambiguous.

☐ Is easy to remember and share.

☐ Is unique and catchy.

☐ Clearly indicates what the book is about.

☐ Would work well as a headline in a newspaper or sales letter.

☐ Is easy to spell and pronounce.

☐ Uses simple, dramatic and/or sensational words.

YOUR SCORE

0-6: Do not put it on your book! This headline will put people to sleep, won't grab attention and will possibly spell instant failure for your book's chances. Ask yourself, "How can I make my title tick more boxes?" It's really worth getting this as good as you can!

7-15: Could be a winner! It really depends *where* you scored highly. If you strongly agreed with just *one* of the first three components of a good book title then it's probably a great title. If you didn't then ask yourself, "How can I make this title tick one of the first 3 boxes?"

16+: You have a killer title! This will be a huge asset to your book and, as you'll see later, will make cashing in on your authority far more lucrative. Whether you self-publish or are looking for a publisher the title alone will be responsible for 80% of the decision making process. If you scored this highly we may want to publish your book so get in touch at *www.bookshaker.com/authors* if you'd like to work with us.

Step 2: Finding A Market For Your Book

"Playing safe is a loser's strategy. If you want the high fruit you've got to shake the tree. Risk your ego – be bold."

Joe Gregory, www.leanmarketing.co.uk

Having a winning idea is a great start but if your book's subject is so obscure as to have a potential readership of just a couple of hundred people then you won't become wealthy from selling your books. This step will ensure you have identified and can access a decent market for your book and can make all the difference between success and failure.

Self Test: Does Your Book Have A Future?

You should be able to tick every single box in this list.

☐ There are at least 3 popular magazines for my book's potential readers.

☐ There are industry statistics clearly showing a market (of at least 100,000 people) exists for my subject area.

☐ My book solves a problem or addresses a need my market actually has.

☐ The market isn't saturated with lots of books that already promise what my book promises and in exactly the same way.

☐ The people in my market actually buy and read books.

☐ There are already other big-selling or best-selling books that hit a similar market to me.

☐ There are definitely people who want it and/or need it.

☐ It solves a problem or facilitates an achievement.

☐ It is unique but still fits neatly into an existing/popular/mature category.

Where's Your Book's Niche?

Finding a niche is another topic that is too often over-complicated by idiots out to make quick money by over-engineering a solution. Quite simply, if your book appeals to 'anyone and everyone' then you don't have a niche:

> *"You have to appeal to 'someone'*
> *to successfully make a connection."*

Use this simple scale to determine your book's niche-ability. You want to get as close to the left as possible and ensure that the 'someone' you're appealing to is made up of enough individual 'some-bodies' to make your niche a profitable one.

SOMEONE								ANYONE

If your book *does* happen to appeal to anyone then don't worry. Make it for 'someone' anyway. You could either produce lots of different versions of the book for different niches or plan ahead to ensure you find the top three niches and focus on selling and marketing to those first. The worst thing you can do is try to sell to everyone because your efforts will be scattered and your effectiveness diluted.

Is Your Book's Niche Topical, Demographical or Both?

There are essentially two ways to choose a niche:

1. **Topic**: The focus of a topically targeted book will be an interest, skill, goal, hobby, sport or specific subject and could potentially attract *any* readers interested in *that* topic. This can be defined more simply as "What the book is about?"

2. **Demographic:** The focus of a demographically targeted book will be experience, age, gender, lifestyle, social group, sexual preference, religion, nationality, ethnicity, income, profession, education etc. By its nature it forces you to generalise about a section of the population so you can make your message resonate with them. This can be defined more simply as "Who is the book for?"

It's possible to niche solely on topic with non-fiction but you can add extra power to your book's proposition if you also identify (and target) a specific demographic too. With fiction however, although not the main focus of this book, the demographic profile will almost always take precedence over the topic. *Harry Potter* wasn't successful because it appealed to 'Wizard Enthusiasts' (it created more of those than existed before it) but because it appealed to the truisms (school, bullying, growing up, making friends etc.) of its demographically targeted audience.

When you're writing a non-fiction book the topic is usually obvious and limited to a few options (based on your expertise and the subject you've identified) but the demographic variations can be huge. So use the following approach to map out your potential targets.

1. Draw a matrix with the various key topics (What) of your book across the top (columns) and the various demographic variables (Who) down the side (rows).

2. If you're having trouble coming up with demographic groups then think about yourself first. Were you a teenage goth or punk? Are you a parent? Are you single? What job do you do? How old are you? Are you a baby-boomer? Are you gay or straight? How much do you earn? What are your religious beliefs? What are your political beliefs? Once you've defined yourself you'll easily be able to find alternatives for other groups. If you're a mum and you run a business and you're planning on writing a book about business for mums you're onto a good niche!

3. Anywhere you get an interesting or appealing combination (in that it will create a unique take on a book) of the 'What' and the 'Who' write a potential book description/title. You don't have to find something for every combination as by doing this you'll realise some demographic targets just wouldn't be right.

4. Here's an example of 3 very different topics to illustrate how this approach works (your own book will probably have tighter topics)...

	TRAVEL	SELF DEFENCE	BUSINESS
BEGINNER	The First Timer's Skiing Holiday	How Not To Hit Like A Geek: Even If You Are	The Business Startup Action Plan
ADVANCED	Off The Beaten Track: Adventurous Holiday Ideas	Peak Performance Training Drills For Martial Artists	Time for Growth: Take Your Business To The Next Level
TEACHER	Peak Season Travel: How To Cut The Cost	Teachers: Stay Safe, Stay Legal	Make Extra Money As A Home Tutor
ENTREPRENEUR	How To Run Your Business... Anywhere	Bare Knuckle Selling: Knockout Sales Tactics	Win The Dragon: How To Get Funding For Your Great Idea
TEEN	The Travelling Teen: Teen-Friendly Travel Destinations	Beat The Bully: Non-Violent Self Defence That Works	How To Make Money While Your Friends Just Spend
MUM	Don't Forget The Kids! How To Enjoy Exotic Holidays With The Kids in Tow	The Way of The Mum: Self Defence To Keep Your Family Safe	The Mumpreneur's Guide To Business Success
STUDENT	Gap Year Traveller: Seeing The World When You're Broke	Stay Safe on Campus: How To Avoid Trouble & Defend Yourself	Student Millionaire: 7 of The Top Internet Businesses Were Started By People Like You!
RETIREE	Top 10 Cruises For The Silver Surfer	Old Dogs Still Bite: Self Defence For The Over 60s	Hobbies That Pay: 101 Ways To Boost Your Retirement Income & Enjoy It
WOMAN	The Worldly Woman's Guide To Safe Solo Travel	Self Defence & The City: The Savvy Woman's Guide To Personal Protection	Bitchy Business: How To Handle Office Politics
GAY MAN	The Gay Guy's Guide To Gay Paris	So Macho! The Gay Guy's Guide To Self Defence	Gay Business Pride: How These Guys Did It & You Can Too
CHRISTIAN	7 Christian Pilgrimages You Should Make In Your Lifetime	The 10 Self Defence Commandments: Protecting Yourself from Violent Attack	What Would Jesus Do? The Christian's Marketing Bible

Do You Really Need A Demographic Niche For Your Book?

Some people would argue that making a book too demographically focused limits the potential for sales. In some cases I'd agree with this and if there is no justifiable reason for defining the demographic then don't do it.

If your book has already been written without an obvious *who* then don't worry. You can still use this matrix to help you decide on a target for your marketing plan. Even a generic self defence book can be made to appeal to a unique demographic (say women) if you focus your publicity effort, articles and press releases on that demographic.

You'll Know Your Niche Is Right When You Hear These Words

To sum this up, if you've niched correctly on both the *what* and the *who* then your readers will be able to say...

> *"It's a book on _____ and it's written for people like me!"*

Self Test: Does Your Book Appeal To Hungry Fanatics?

If you're still not sure how to define a niche then use this simple, but powerful, checklist. If you can tick every box then you will have found a good source of hungry fanatics who will love your book.

☐ Your ideal reader is easily identifiable by age, gender, nationality, education-level or other demographic attribute.

☐ Your ideal reader has a very specific interest or need (a sport like football, a thing like jewellery, a hobby like sailing, a self improvement goal like getting published, a business like consulting or a need like getting out of debt).

☐ Your ideal reader has money and is willing to spend money (usually much more than the cost of your book) on fulfilling their need/want.

☐ There are other people/companies successfully selling things to your target reader already (magazines, books, DVDs, information products, memberships, training courses etc.)

☐ Your ideal reader hangs out with others just like them in places that are easy for you to find and access (associations, online networks, offline networks, trade shows, clubs etc.)

☐ You have something that they will really love because it a) solves a real problem for them that nobody else has solved, b) gives them what they want, but better than anyone else is giving it, c) meets their needs/wants in a unique or exciting way, d) is new to them.

Quick & Dirty Ways To Do Book Market Research

I'll keep repeating this because it's important. The longer you linger at the research stage the longer it will take for your book to bring in any profit. Don't get me wrong, making sure there's a market is very important! But, given that the greatest book market research tool is now freely available to everyone with an internet connection, you don't have to over-engineer a solution and write a thesis in order to know if your book is commercially viable. So, with that in mind, here are some quick and dirty strategies to determine your book's potential market.

A Free Tool For Tracking Market Trends

This approach will give you a really good feel for how popular a particular subject is in relation to other similar topics and whether it's a growth area. Here's what you do...

1. Go to *www.google.com/trends*
2. Choose a keyword or phrase related to your book's main theme/topic.
3. Use the dropdowns to select specific geographic regions and timeframes.
4. Separate multiple search terms with a comma to compare them directly with one another.

A Free Search Engine For Finding Popular Blogs & Topics

The benefit of doing this is that if there are lots of people blogging on a subject and lots of people interested in their posts then you'll have a great target of well connected influencers to give review copies of your book to when it comes to promoting it. Tim Ferris, bestselling author of *The 4-Hour Workweek* befriended bloggers and got their support to help make his book a huge success.

1. Go to *www.technorati.com*
2. Click the 'Popular' tag and see what's hot right now.
3. Use the tabs to further search by things like news, movies and books.
4. You can also use the keyword search to find blogs and posts on your topic and use this to gauge what people are interested in and the potential for finding connectors when it's time to promote your book.

A Free & Powerful Tool For Gauging A Book's Market Size

Google provides you with some fantastically powerful tools and they're free! I can't go into detail on every aspect of Google Adwords here but I highly recommend you buy and read *Adwords for Dummies* (the most recent edition you can because Google changes often) by Howie Jacobson. For now though...

1. Go to *www.google.com/adwords*
2. Sign up as an advertiser (this will come in handy when it's time for promotion anyway).
3. You now have access to tools that will show how many people searched for a particular term, phrase or topic in the last month and how many advertisers are competing for that particular word or phrase.
4. Essentially you'll have a useful number to make an educated guess on the total market and you'll be able to see whether other people (advertisers) are making an income from serving it.

The Greatest Book Marketing Research Tool Ever ... and It's Free

You probably use this tool every day but you may not have thought of it as a market research tool until now. Of course I'm talking about Amazon. You can sort by keywords and best-seller lists on specific subjects, you can sort other author's books by sales rank, you can uncover what's wrong with the competition and, when you know where to look, you can even make a good guess about how many copies a title is selling.

1. Go to *www.amazon.com* or *www.amazon.co.uk* if you know you're only planning on targeting the UK.

2. Use Amazon's search bar to look for competitors (it ranks them by most popular by default).

3. Also use the categories section to see what's popular in various more general subject areas.

4. Click on books that are doing well for a similar topic/audience to yours.

5. Check the overall Sales Rank of these books. If a book is in the top 2,000 for sales rank over a period of time then assume it's bringing in a decent monthly income.

6. If none of the books catering to your same target/topic are ranked this highly then you've either found an opportunity to provide something really good in this category or there isn't much of a market and you may need to rethink.

If you find a real star in your area then look at the following things (I'd even go so far as to buy the book to do this) and be prepared to model them:

✓ Check out the cover – what's the big promise? What's the title? Does it look professional or funky? Cluttered or simple? Academic or Accessible?

✓ Check out the blurb – who's the book pitched at? Novice/Advanced?

- ✓ Check out the 'Look Inside' and review the Table of Contents, Reviews, Foreword or any other keys to why the book is doing well.

- ✓ Check out the price – is it priced for mass market appeal or is it priced high? What discount is Amazon offering? A high discount means the publisher may be 'buying' sales by giving away a bigger chunk of the profit to retailers.

All of this competitive research will give you useful data to enable you to differentiate your book, price it correctly (you could average the top 10 books on your subject to do this), set your discount and ensure your book isn't missing any tricks.

How To Research The Market While You Build A List

As you'll already know I have a pretty simple rule that I like to live by...

"There's usually an easy way and a hard way to do something. Always pick the easy one first."

Joe Gregory, www.leanmarketing.co.uk

With that in mind I'm going to encourage you to do two jobs for the price of one by showing you how to do some market research while simultaneously building a list of prospective buyers when your book is ready to go. Here's how you do it:

1. Make sure you've identified your target reader (using the Hungry Fanatics self test earlier in this chapter).

2. If you don't already have one then set up an account with an email list management provider that can also send auto-responders. For professional use we recommend *www.aweber.com* or *www.getresponse.com* (which are really powerful but charge monthly fees) but for now, something simple and free will work like *www.freeautobot.com*

3. Create the bait. Create a special report, unique article or useful checklist for your target that is strongly related to (but not exactly like) the subject of your book (as an

example we provided a free Business Card Design report to build leads for our *Gorillas Want Bananas* book because they both target small and new business owners).

4. Create a page to advertise your freebie and include a signup form (provided by your email provider) promising to send subscribers a copy of the report by email (which is what you'll give them in the autoresponder).

5. Find a place your prospective target hangs out, an online network, Facebook club, forum etc and offer the freebie.

6. Check your results. How many people were in the network approached you? How many people downloaded the freebie? What percentage of that closed group were interested?

7. Once you get a snapshot (you really need to test your offer in a network with at least 1,000 prospective readers) extrapolate the figures based on the total reachable target market (which you can estimate using Google's free adword tools) and your percentage of the test group.

The LEP Test: Is The Market Likely To Pay Enough?

Once you've got useful data about your market using the tools detailed earlier and you've done a live marketing experiment by offering a test freebie it's time to turn this into a number you can use to decide if the market is right. Here's how...

1. Total Estimated Market Size X Freebie Response % = BEST CASE SALES (BCS)

2. BCS X Profit Per Book (PBB) = Market's *Maximum* Earning Potential (MEP)

3. MEP X 0.25 Hassle/Saturation Factor = *Likely* Earning Potential (LEP)

4. If this figure (LEP) doesn't look good to you then it's the wrong book for the wrong market.

5. Sometimes there are many potential markets for a single book (see the earlier piece on Topical and Demographical niching) so pick the best paying one first and only look at others once 80% of your LEP has been reached or until sales to that target begin to dry up.

What Makes Your Book Better Than The Rest?

"If you can't join them – beat them!"

Debbie Jenkins, www.leanmarketing.co.uk

It's important to know how your book idea will sit amongst the competition. You don't want to be stuck in the anonymity of me-too so use this tool to stake your claim on those over-crowded bookshelves.

I'd suggest comparing your book against the top 3-5 books in your category using your research on Amazon and your experience of these books (if you've read them – which I recommend) to plot how they meet readers' needs on the following chart.

Your goal is to plot benefits and features offered by the various books and look for gaps that are important to your audience but aren't being met. You can then to *use* these gaps to positively differentiate your book.

Once you've identified how your book is better you need to include this information in all of your marketing material. That includes the book's sales blurb, introduction, your website and anywhere else potential readers may be looking.

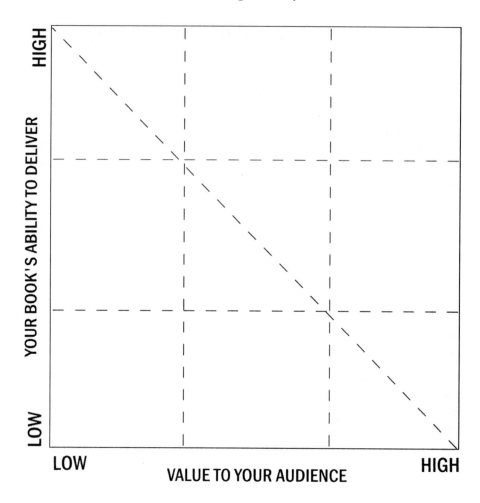

Here's an example of how we ensured *The Wealthy Author* could stake a claim against some stiff competition. We consider the books we compared ourselves against to be the best in the market and strongly recommend that you buy and read them all. In fact all of them are stronger than this book in certain areas (not necessarily on this chart) but by identifying the things we deemed to be *most* important to our audience we made our book shine where it counts.

BENEFITS WE COMPARED

1. Write A Book Quickly & Easily
2. Get Your Book Published

3. Sell Loads of Books
4. Become Wealthy From Books

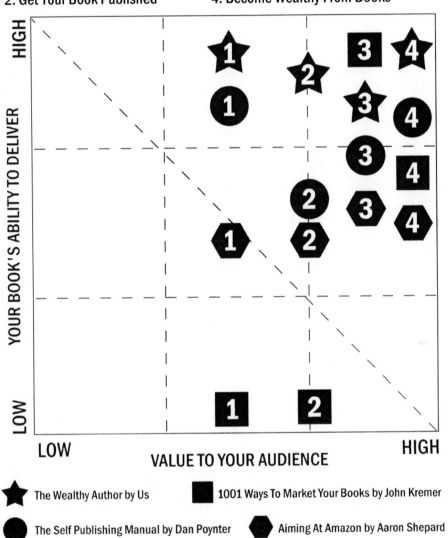

Step 3: Getting Your Book Written

"Creativity is often over-rated. Sometimes success calls for a bit of humble productivity."

Joe Gregory, www.leanmarketing.co.uk

I've said it before and I'll say it again, the writing is the easy part of being an author. That is, as long as you've set things up to go in your favour and you're genuinely qualified to be writing the book in the first place.

The Easy Way To Write A Non-Fiction Book

There is almost always a hard way and an easy way to do things so why not choose the easy one? Here are the essential steps to writing your book the easy way.

1. Ensure you know your book's overall approach – see The 6 Most Common Non-Fiction Book Archetypes (later in this chapter) for more on this.

2. Choose a voice and tone for your book – friendly, ranting, encouraging etc. so you can stay in character throughout.

3. Map out your entire book visually so you can see any gaps in the overall content and ensure you're not missing anything important.

4. Know how many words you're aiming for and work out how many words each chapter should contain, on average, to create the whole book.

5. Decide on and stick to a consistent set of rules such as: hyphenation, spellings, heading levels, chapter structure etc. – see Your Non-Fiction Book Blueprint and Style Rules (also later in this chapter) for more information.

6. Use the CRI method (I'll explain that shortly) to write each chapter step-by-step.

7 Tips For Writing A Better Book

- ✓ Make A Big Promise & Deliver
- ✓ Use Simple Language
- ✓ Make it Clear
- ✓ Know Your Audience
- ✓ Write How You Speak
- ✓ Write Your Book Like A Series of Articles
- ✓ End Your Book With A Bang

Make A Big Promise & Deliver On It

If your book doesn't excite your reader and tell them why they should invest the next 12 hours of their life reading it then you're missing a trick.

I like to think of a book as an infomercial...

- ✓ It's got to have a hook and reason to keep watching.
- ✓ It's got to tell people something they don't already know.
- ✓ It's got to talk about the benefits to them first and the features only where necessary.
- ✓ It's got to make you look clever.
- ✓ It's got to have a call to action.

What do you want people to do with your book anyway? Ignoring all the far reaching things like, "sharing my message with the world", "improving the lives of my readers" or "creating a legacy", the bottom line for a wealthy author is this...

> *"You want people to buy your book.*
> *If they don't then you don't get paid"*

Debbie Jenkins, www.leanmarketing.co.uk

If they don't buy your book then they can't read it (unless they borrow it or steal it – the blaggers) either. You want people to read your book because if they don't then you don't get to achieve any of your loftier goals and they don't get to see how great you are.

If you start your book without a hook (people look at the front matter and blurb to decide if the book's for them) then you're going to have a hard job convincing anyone to buy it let alone convincing them to read it. So do yourself a favour and make a big promise – or lots of promises – and then deliver on them throughout the book. Your readers will love you for it and your book will actually get read instead of gathering dust in a clearance bin.

Use Simple Language

If there's a hard way or an easy way to say something then use the easy way. Some authors make a sport out of finding more and more obscure words and acronyms to describe stuff that's essentially simple. So, if you do need to use an obscure word then be sure to include a glossary or, better still, provide a definition with its first use.

If, however, you're only using big words in an attempt to baffle readers with your intellect and look clever then stop it. For starters, nobody likes a smart arse! Plus you'll look like a self-conscious and self-important jerk while alienating many of your readers.

For me (and Bruce Lee as it happens) the height of sophistication is simplicity. So *be clever* by using simple words rather than trying to *look clever* by using a thesaurus to come up with more and more obscure ways to say a simple thing because any fool can do the latter.

Make it Clear

Closely related to using simple language is the importance of making things clear. Never say something in three steps if it can be said just as easily in one. This is just creating filler and, while it makes your book bigger, it can bore your readers to the point of unconsciousness.

If you have a really important point to make then explain it a few different ways to ensure you've been absolutely clear but then move on. Give your readers some credit.

Also, if a simple tool, series of bullet points or a clear image can say things that would otherwise take you ten pages to explain then include them. You can still include the ten pages of detail after but at least the reader has a model (or a visual aid) to refer to while you ramble.

Finally, don't mix your metaphors. If you're talking about 'ballpark figures' then don't also put 'the writing on the wall' and mention that 'somebody's boat has just come in'. See what I have to say about clichés shortly and you'll avoid most of these traps anyway.

Know Your Audience

Are you aiming for beginners or experts? Is your audience likely to be made up of lay people or science boffins?

Covering all the basics in a book for boffins will bore them into oblivion so consider including the basics in a reference section, refer them to simpler books or make it clear this stuff is here as a refresher. Likewise, assuming that your reader knows all the basics and then talking about difficult stuff without covering the basics first will alienate the reader.

Make it clear who your book is for (and what level of skill or knowledge you're assuming they have) from the outset and it will make your job of writing the book easier. It will free you from having to 'dumb down' your advanced information and you can focus on creating a book your readers will love. It will also allow you to skip the more complicated stuff while ensuring your readers feel they're getting what you promised.

If in doubt then cover the essential basics first and excuse yourself by explaining that many readers will know this already so they can skip it.

Write How You Speak

Very talented people who try to write a book often think they absolutely must get all of the grammar right and use a thesaurus to come up with a hundred synonyms for the same word or they'll look foolish.

Instead of just getting on with it they start using big words they would never say and tie themselves up like Houdini in an attempt to sound professional and clever. But it fails. The writing comes across as self-conscious and the reader will often feel embarrassed by the author's fumbling attempts to impress.

Just stop a moment and think about it. Most people read a book because they want the information it contains or, more specifically, the benefits it promises. If what you're writing is easily understandable, unambiguous and easy to read then I'd argue you've achieved that goal. I'm almost certain that this book is full of grammatical cock ups and goofs (plenty that I insisted remained despite my editor's pleading) because I write pretty much how I speak. This will annoy some people but what *they* think of my grammar really doesn't keep me up at night.

While it's true that some people are hyper-critical about grammar that's really their own personal fetish and not something you should seriously worry about. I won't go into the detail (because it's pretty boring) but grammar typically falls into 'prescriptive' (what the rule-makers and grammar-geeks would like to see) and 'descriptive' (what people actually do and say). Using the former to beat people up for doing what falls under the latter is stupid because language is always evolving.

Here's why you should ignore the 'grammar police' and write how you (or at least people like you) speak...

- ✓ It engages the reader by not patronising or talking down to them.
- ✓ It allows your personality to shine through – okay that's not always a benefit if you're short on personality.
- ✓ It's easier to write (you can always get a good editor to make sense of your ramblings later if you're scared of getting picked on by the 'grammar-geeks', so don't worry).
- ✓ It often results in clearer and less convoluted sentences and fewer big (or obscure) words. Your reader shouldn't have to constantly refer to their dictionary when they'd be better off just reading your book.

Write Your Book Like It's A Series of Articles

Check this book's contents page and you'll see a pattern. It reads like a series of articles on all kinds of subjects that authors and would-be authors will be interested in. This is not a happy accident but a deliberate design feature, because...

- ✓ I now have a whole library of stuff I can cherry pick and repurpose as articles and press releases to promote *The Wealthy Author.*
- ✓ The contents page (something almost everyone checks out before buying a book) becomes a very powerful selling tool in its own right.
- ✓ The contents page (and all the headings in the book) will be packed with relevant keywords that help it get picked up in search engines (like *http://books.google.com*) and online bookstores (like *www.amazon.com*).
- ✓ Each chapter is easy to write with a clear focus because I'm writing the book one article at a time.
- ✓ If you follow our advice for cashing in on your authority in Step 6 you'll realise you've now got loads of ready-made content that's easy to repackage (essentially recycle) in different formats to make more money.

End Your Book With A Bang

TV shows, movies, live bands and Broadway musicals all end with a big finale because they want people to applaud and leave feeling absolutely great. It doesn't necessarily matter if the show was 80% junk because, as long as the beginning and the ending is good, most people will believe it was a success. So why do most non-fiction books simply end with a pop and a fizzle if you're lucky or an abrupt stop if you're not?

While I don't know the answer to this question I do know that the authors of these books are missing a trick. Here's how to end with a bang...

- ✓ Remind people of all the cool stuff they learned with a big summary (it will also help sell copies too, as prospective readers often go to the back to have a quick skim before buying).

- ✓ Tell them how to think and feel now they've successfully completed your book. Simply telling people that they can feel smug, pleased with themselves, happy, relieved or proud will get that very response in most cases.
- ✓ So, once you've reminded them of all the cool stuff you just shared and you've told them they can feel great about how much better their life is now they've read your book you can also tell them what to do next.
- ✓ In marketing we call this your MWR (Most Wanted Response) so, while they're enjoying their 'high' from finishing your book you can lead them somewhere (perhaps to a sign up form on your website) where they'll get an additional free bonus. See the back of this book for yours.

Write Your Book Without Tears Using The CRI System

"The faster I fail, the quicker I learn. Don't wait until everything is 100% perfect to take action!"

Joe Gregory, www.leanmarketing.co.uk

Once you've mapped out your entire book it's often a good idea to treat each chapter as a unique project in its own right. I also like to write each chapter using these 3 distinct steps, doing one at a time and not all at once. This is what I suggest you do on a chapter-by-chapter basis – remember to CRI…

1. **Create** – keep writing as if your life depended on it – limit your self-editing and internal critic in order to produce the quantity of content you require.

2. **Review** – once you've written everything down, read through and spot for any gaps, inconsistencies or obvious errors and make notes – either directly in your manuscript or in a notebook. Double-check the word count and if you need to remove stuff then cut it and paste it into a separate 'brain dump' file. The stuff you cut from your main book may still come in handy later as inspiration for an article, press release or content for another chapter.

3. **Improve** – start at the beginning of the chapter again and, using your notes, go back through to add, remove, re-order or improve upon the content. Then stop. The chapter is done for now!

The Writing Process Chapter-by-Chapter

"Stop Starting and Start Stopping!"

Debbie Jenkins, www.leanmarketing.co.uk

1. Add in all the headings and sub-headings for the chapter (see Mapping Out Your Book for more information).

2. Go back to the start and write a chapter introduction (which should spell out what people are going to learn and set the scene).

3. If you know how many words each chapter should contain then you need to divide this between the headings (it doesn't have to be divided equally but it will help you avoid over-writing if you have a target in mind). You may find it easier to convert your word count into a page count by first working out the average number of words each page contains and then dividing this by the number of words available for each chapter.

4. Treat each heading as a unique standalone article and write the content for each one using the T^4 'Tell Them Tell Them' Format in other words...

    a. Tell them what you're going to tell them. Give the big picture and/or set the scene.

    b. Tell them. Add in more detail and, where possible, lead them onto the next point for extra polish.

5. If you need to clarify a point with a chart, table or illustration then make a note of what you want in a typeface that stands out – but keep on writing.

6. Once you've finished writing it's time to review and improve (CRI) and then move onto the next chapter.

4 Essential Things To Include In A Non-Fiction Book

All non-fiction books should contain the following:

- ✓ Praise
- ✓ Acknowledgements
- ✓ Foreword/Introduction
- ✓ Author Biography

Praise

Otherwise known as social proof, you can never have enough of this stuff because it's one of the most persuasive pieces of marketing content your prospective buyers will read. What other people say about you is always taken more seriously by your potential readers than what you say about yourself!

You'll be relying on other people to get back to you though, so I'd start soliciting praise as soon as possible. While you can't expect people to write praise for a book that's not written yet you can still get in touch with people you really admire or trust and ask them to agree to 'take a look' and write something for your book before it goes to print.

Good praise will say specific things about how your book solves a problem, makes people think differently or could change the reader's life in some tangible way. There are ways to ask for praise that will ensure you get good stuff.

If you're writing a book on something you've been doing for a long time (your business or a skill you have) then there's absolutely nothing wrong with including 'praise for the author' from your clients and people who've benefited from your advice over the years too.

We'll look at the specifics of how to ask for praise and get endorsements later, in Step 5, but for now just know it's an essential part of a good book, so it needs to be done right up front.

Acknowledgements

Some authors like to show off their creativity here and come up with a witty little acknowledgements page. While this is often the most enjoyable approach for the reader I believe it misses the point. This is your best chance to gain new supporters and acknowledge the people who've helped you so far. It's also your opportunity to 'chat up' your fellow authors, heroes and anyone else who has helped (or who you'd like to help you) to make your book succeed.

✓ Thank the reader and your intended target audience as a whole. Flatter them a bit (do it tongue in cheek if you like) for being so clever and brilliant and better than the rest for having chosen to read your book. This can also further reinforce who your book is for and what they'll get.

✓ Thank people who generally helped: your publisher (especially if you're hoping to publish more books with them), editor (even if you paid them a fortune), designer (likewise), proof reader, friends, person who wrote a foreword, people who gave you praise etc. Where possible you should include their website address. Family may come into this list too but if you're using this tactically then I'd mention your partner, kids, mother and father etc. in a dedication instead.

✓ Thank people who inspire you: this can include other authors and even big names. There's nothing wrong, for instance, in saying something like, "I really want to thank Tony Robbins for challenging me to make my goals even bigger." Unless you're not a fan! I'd always include a website link where possible too so they gain a tangible benefit from the mention. The benefit of this is two-fold:

o Social proof/authority by association – the reader now cannot help but associate you with your hero and also it's ambiguous whether you know the big man more personally, so they could also believe you're one of his buddies.

o You've acknowledged someone very powerfully who would be a useful ally in the future. When it comes time to ask for a little endorsement or mention to their contacts, then their name in your book will make them more inclined to like you.

✓ Thank people who've provided you or are planning to provide you with marketing support. Again include web links to these people. They could include bloggers, fellow authors, journalists and any other well connected people who are willing to help.

Foreword/Introduction

A good introduction is a really important part of any book. Sometimes it's worth having both a Foreword and an Introduction because the Foreword (which is usually written by someone else) may not spell out everything your reader needs to know to decide to buy my book.

If you're having galleys (pre publication mock-ups) done or using print on demand (where it's easy to include a foreword after the book is in print) then wait until you have something solid and real you can send before asking for a foreword. If you really need to go to print and you're going to have a large run of books then you need to get this earlier and you may need to send an electronic version of the book to your foreword writer.

A Good Foreword Should:

✓ Be written by a known name, authority, celebrity that your readers and prospective readers will know, admire and trust.

✓ Focus on the benefits of your book to the reader from the perspective of the authority writing it.

✓ Make reference to why the foreword writer is qualified to comment on, and recommend the advice in, your book.

A Good Introduction Should:

✓ Summarise what readers are going to get from reading your book:

   ✓ What they'll learn

   ✓ How they'll feel

   ✓ What they'll experience

- ✓ Make explicit your book's big promise.
- ✓ Give readers a rough idea where they'll find the answers and information they might be seeking.
- ✓ Give an overview of the book and what's where (sometimes it's worth writing this as a special 'how to use this book' if you have specific instructions).

Author Biography

This is the place to really lay on your credentials. Ask yourself, "Why am I uniquely qualified to write this book and why should readers listen to what I have to say?"

Some people write a whole résumé here but it's much better if you can tell them a story where you either overcame an obstacle or stumbled upon the secrets you're sharing in the book.

Finally, weave things in like how long you've been an expert on your subject, how much money you've made, how many TV, radio and magazine appearances you've got and all the rest of the stuff that lets readers know you're an authority.

The 6 Most Common Non-Fiction Archetypes

"Learn from great people but don't worship them. Nobody's that great except you!"

Joe Gregory, www.leanmarketing.co.uk

Even in the realm of non-fiction there are various common themes you can use to define the type of book being written. The following list of archetypes is by no means exhaustive but it does give you one more thing you can get clear on before you begin to write. And, as you already know, the less thinking you have to do when you should be writing the easier it is to write your book.

Archetype 1: The Factual How To Book

This type of book usually deals with self help, sports or hobbies where the details are not likely to change very quickly (i.e. they relate to stable subjects and not rapidly advancing trends) and the facts are pretty much widely accepted.

Examples: Psychology & Relationships, Martial Arts (Judo, Karate, Boxing etc.) & Athletics (Swimming, Running etc.), Selling & Persuasion, Motivation & Inspiration, Spirituality & Superstition, most Self Help (especially dealing with goals and success), Dancing & Music, Mainstream (and accepted) Science etc.

Pros:

- ✓ Long shelf life (doesn't need constant revisions).
- ✓ Solves problems / offers solutions / gives useful information.
- ✓ Easy to define target market and identify competitors.

Cons:

- ✗ Can be difficult to differentiate your book because the facts are pretty much the same so you can't write a whole lot of new stuff.
- ✗ Competition is often high as older and well-liked books will still be relevant in a mature category.
- ✗ Unless you can find a way to present your book in a contentious and attention grabbing way you haven't got a very news-worthy book.

Consider:

- ✓ Reader sophistication – a book for beginners will be very different to one for experts on many of these subjects. If there is a steep learning curve then it may be better to create a series of books to cover each stage.
- ✓ To overcome the differentiation problem it's worth seeing if you can present the information in a new and exciting way or find one existing paradigm and disagree with it.
- ✓ Packaging your book to stand out from the other books in this category.

Archetype 2: The Technical Tutorial Book

This type of book typically deals with very specific subjects where the details are important and the facts continue to evolve over time, and often change very quickly, if not constantly.

Examples: Law & Medicine, Software Tutorials, Programming, Web Applications, Technology, Trends, Care Repair Manuals.

Pros:

- ✓ If you can build a loyal reader base for this type of book then you can re-sell them the same content (with a few updates) each year without fear of competing with your older and now defunct editions.
- ✓ Easy to define target market & identify competitors.
- ✓ You can ride the wave of popularity around a subject or technology (there are loads of social media books coming out as I write this and some of them will be winners as people are hungry for *any* information they can get their hands on).
- ✓ If you already know how to do the thing you're writing a book on then it's easy, you just write it down step-by-step.

Cons:

- ✗ Standards, technologies and rules change so the book will go out of date very quickly (and will usually need yearly revisions).
- ✗ Short shelf life (needs regular revisions which could mean lots of unsold stock and a yearly task to revise the book).
- ✗ A high-risk book with a small time-window to make a return and a risk that information could be out of date by the time it goes to print.
- ✗ You're dealing with facts so it's not the easiest book to inject personality, contentiousness or newsworthiness into, which could give you a hard job with the marketing.
- ✗ The subject and not the author is the real star so it's hard to build back-end kudos for yourself from this kind of book (which is why they're usually written by a panel of experts instead).

✘ Some technologies completely die so, say if you'd written a book on HD-DVD instead of BluRay you could find yourself with a book with no market very quickly.

✘ The edit will often require someone with both editing and technical skills related to the subject, increasing the cost and time involved in this phase.

Consider:

✓ Reader sophistication – a book for beginners will be very different to one for experts on many of these subjects. If there is a steep learning curve then it may be better to create a series of books to cover each stage.

✓ Minimising your exposure to risk by looking at producing very light, magazine-style books and selling them as an updatable series instead.

✓ Avoiding this type of book entirely! If you're up against larger, wealthier publishers and authors who won't be as badly affected by the risks then you've got a real fight on your hands.

✓ If you're an author looking for a mainstream publishing contract then accept this as a one-off-payment commission only. Your chances of making any money in royalties over the long term from this type of book are very low, so it's not the best model for wealthy authors (who look for long term royalties) but fine for jobbing writers.

Archetype 3: The Complete Reference or Guide Book

This type of book covers a broad range of information on a specific topic but doesn't necessarily try to educate or have a particular logic or flow to it. It's simply a reference containing useful information that people can dip into easily at any time.

Examples: Travel Guide, Directory, Dictionary/Encyclopaedia (often on a subject like marketing), Language Guide, Quotations, Contacts, Technical Terms (sailing, neurolinguistic programming, psychology, medicine etc.)

Pros:

- ✓ Can often provide advertising revenue up front (and in excess of sales revenue) if you build this into the model.
- ✓ Once you have a loyal following you can re-sell them the same basic book (with updated information) year after year.
- ✓ It's easy to write because you can simply dump all the relevant information into specific sections without having to worry about taking readers through a logical and well-planned process or journey.
- ✓ Reference books can always find an audience where there's a great deal of how to books, so can sometimes be a way to differentiate your book and find a niche within a popular area.

Cons:

- ✗ You're dealing with facts so it's not the easiest book to inject personality, contentiousness or newsworthiness into, which could give you a hard job with the marketing.
- ✗ Reference books are very research intensive and accuracy is important to the reader. So if you don't check your sources carefully you'll get negative reviews which will undermine the reliability of the entire book.
- ✗ Rarely takes readers on a journey (they'll just dip in for stuff they want) which makes it harder for you to genuinely impact their thinking.
- ✗ Doesn't increase the author's authority because it's just a collection of researched information. Plus you'll be up against plenty of free sources for the same information.
- ✗ The edit will often require someone with both editing and technical skills related to the subject, increasing the cost and time involved in this phase.
- ✗ Can be difficult to differentiate your book because the facts are pretty much the same so you can't write a whole lot of new stuff.
- ✗ To do a reference book properly you should employ the services of a professional indexer. This adds extra cost.

Consider:

- ✓ Finding information is a really important feature of a reference book's success so get a proper index done (using a professional indexer if you have the funds) and include lots of glossaries, visual maps and other tools to make finding information easier. This may be the only thing you can use to differentiate yourself from other books covering the same stuff.

- ✓ Focus on beating other reference books by being able to say yes to one or more of the following:

    a. The most comprehensive – wider number of "entries" or "deeper definitions/entries" or both.

    b. The best indexed – easier to find stuff fast.

    c. The most up-to-date – you'll have to keep bringing new editions out regularly to keep this advantage, so perhaps not so good as the other two.

Archetype 4: Observational/Critical/Social Commentary

Some books are very successful despite often just telling us what we already know. They typically set out to answer or provide an explanation to one of life's big (or even small but universal) questions.

Examples: it's harder to generalise with this category so I'll get specific: *The Luck Factor* by Richard Wiseman (why are lucky people luckier), *Making Time* (why does time appear to pass at different speeds), *The Tipping Point* by Malcolm Gladwell (how epidemics and pandemics of all kinds happen), *Why Men Don't Listen and Women Can't Read Maps* by Allan & Barbara Pease (enough said!), *Influence* by Robert Cialdini (how people manage to get us to do stuff even if we didn't want to).

Pros:

- ✓ 90% of the book can rely on telling people truisms or observations about what's happening. Telling people what they already know, believe or have experienced to be true.

- ✓ Human nature (and our tendency to look for information that supports our beliefs and ignore the other stuff) means a book that agrees with the reader (even if it's stupid) is often likely to get good reviews from that same reader.

✓ Your book, if well written, will be media friendly and packed with quotable stuff with a wide interest so you'll have an easier job getting people to feature your book and press releases.

✓ Even if your eventual answer (or hypothesis for an answer) to the big question is shaky, you'll gain a following and create contention. This is good for your raising your media profile and will help set you up as an expert.

Cons:

✗ To give your factual stuff credibility it's better if you can back it up with statistics, reports and interesting experiments, this will increase your research time and cost unless you're a nerd (or an academic) and already have a loads of source material.

✗ If you don't make your points convincingly or interestingly enough you could end up writing the world's most boring, obvious and patronising book!

Consider:

✓ The more published studies you can find to support these truisms the better, so it's worth doing your research so readers can feel even more validated in believing this stuff!

✓ Running your own studies, Cialdini and Richard Wiseman did loads, increases perceived authority and also makes you infinitely more quotable in other books and news stories!

✓ Picking on stuff that people feel passionately about will ensure you have a target market and your book will get picked up by connectors in the media.

✓ Watching any good stand up comedians and seeing how they turn mundane daily occurrences into something entertaining, memorable and interesting.

✓ Looking for ways to answer (or at least provide your own viable hypothesis for answering) life's big unanswerable questions – like why are some people luckier than others etc.

- ✓ Learning about Ericksonian Hypnosis, in particular the stuff on 'pacing the client's ongoing reality', to hone your skills as the master of telling people stuff they'll readily agree with! I recommend *Trance-Formations* by Richard Bandler and John Grinder if you can get your hands on a copy

- ✓ If you've got the qualifications PhD or Dr include them with your credit on the title or find a Dr to endorse your book for added kudos.

Archetype 5: The Impassioned Rant, Exposé or Manifesto

Remember the cheeky kid in school who always gave a smart-ass answer to the teacher? If that was you then congratulations you'll be good at this type of book! If it wasn't then be honest, wouldn't you have loved to tell the teacher what they could do with their homework just once? Didn't you secretly admire the kid that always ended up in detention? Books that are critical of something that many people hate will attract fans in their scores. Reading a book like this can be cathartic (somebody else is railing against the accepted wisdom and authority), validating (an authority agrees with you) and/or interesting.

Examples: Again rather than generalising here are some specific examples... *Bad Science* by Ben Goldacre (why do people believe all the BS about health and science in the media), *Sham* by Steve Salerno (how the self help industry keeps us helpless), *No Logo* by Naomi Klein (an impassioned backlash against the multi-national corporations), *The God Delusion* by Richard Dawkins (arming plenty of atheists with the reasoning tools and examples to batter their religious friends around the head), *Con Tricks* by Martin Ashford (how management consultants rip off their clients).

Pros:

- ✓ This kind of book will be extremely media friendly, quotable and packed with contentious stuff so getting people to feature your book and press releases should be really easy.

✓ 90% of the book can rely on telling people truisms or observations about what's happening. Telling people what they already know, believe or have experienced to be true.

✓ Human nature (and our tendency to look for information that supports our beliefs and ignore the other stuff) means a book that agrees with the reader (even if it's stupid) is often likely to get good reviews from that same reader.

✓ Even if your eventual answer (or hypothesis for an answer) to the big question is shaky, you'll gain a following and create contention. This is good for your raising your media profile and will help set you up as an expert!

Cons:

✗ This is a high-risk book to write, but with high risk there is often a bigger reward.

✗ If you pick on specific people, organisations or religions with particularly sensitive and scary factions then your book will sit uneasily with many publishers because they don't want to be sued, blown up or worse!

✗ You need thick skin for this type of book. You'll get attacked, threatened, picked on and chastised by anyone who disagrees with you. So, if you always feared a reprimand from the teacher and the thought of detention still scares you then you may not be cut out for the backlash that will occur.

✗ If your arguments are flimsy and easily intellectually demolished you'll simply look like a ranting nutter and lose a lot of credibility. So, again, it's a high risk strategy.

Consider:

✓ Take a strong, uncompromising stance in favour of or against something or (ideally) both!

✓ Choosing a subject you're passionate about or believe completely. The rant requires the author to take an opinionated and fanatical stance and even if there is balance leave that for the scientists and academics. You'll be more newsworthy if you can ignore the balance and make things as black and white as possible!

✓ Writing under a pseudonym, while it's braver to write under your real name some things aren't worth dying over and if you're ranting against stuff that really matters you will often piss off some pretty crazy groups of fanatical people. Salmon Rushdie for instance is a very brave man but he still has lots of crazy people who want to kill him!

Archetype 6: The 'Feel Good' Inspiration Book

Probably the most insipid of the many common archetypes but there's definitely a market for this stuff. And if you feel that this is where your calling leads you then good luck. It differs from true self-help in the fact that it gives a lot more of the 'what and why' than the 'how'. As you can probably tell I'm not a fan of this kind of book because, unless it's backed up with solid, usable and practical stuff to do, it only provides people with an intellectual painkiller that keeps them stupid while the author benefits. Read *Sham* (a book I mentioned earlier) if you want to know more about why I personally don't like these books. However, my personal beliefs about this type of book shouldn't get in the way of the fact that there's lots of money to be made from it.

Examples: Any of the (hugely popular) *Chicken Soup for the Soul* books, *The Secret* (made worse because it passes off hope as a useful 'how to' strategy), *The Little Book of Calm* (although it's a fun gift with cult status thanks to the TV series *Black Books*), any book by Deepak Chopra, pretty much any book in the Mind, Body and Spirit section of the bookstore.

Pros:

✓ Telling people that what they want most in the world is really easy to achieve never ceases to draw in willing punters and so you should be able to sell a lot of books if you get the marketing right. It's the age-old trick of selling picks to prospectors; the pick seller is the real winner!

✓ There's a lot of money to be made from events, seminars, audios and home-study courses on this stuff, so it's a great way to build longer term wealth into your book's model (more on this in Step 6).

✓ Recession proof! When things are bad these books sell better as people look for answers and hope. When things are good people aspire to even greater heights and look for quick fixes and easy ways to get more 'good stuff'.

✓ Often timeless, these kinds of books typically deal with universal laws and ancient wisdom and therefore will stay relevant (or is that *irrelevant*) for a long time!

✓ The media loves this kind of stuff so, with the right packaging (for you and your book), you can get lots of coverage and raise your profile.

✓ If you run a coaching company or live events then this kind of book will work really well to attract clients.

Cons:

✗ If you have a conscience and you know you're cashing in by offering unsubstantial and often unsubstantiated advice to people who really need help then don't blame me if you have trouble sleeping at night.

✗ Where there's lots of money to be made you'll always find lots of competition. There are a few gurus that really dominate here and, despite their personable and friendly image, they are tough and savvy business people.

✗ Success here is often more of a beauty-pageant than really about the content. So if you're ugly (ie you've got a great face for radio), awkward in social situations, uncharismatic or have a funny voice (and not just because it's exotic and foreign) you should stick to writing something that can stand on its own merit.

✗ Many people, me included, will class you as a snake oil salesman (or woman) but that's only a negative if you care what people like me think of you.

Consider:

✓ Tapping into the extremes of human nature like laziness, wishful thinking, narcissism, jealousy, unhappiness, wanting more etc.

✓ Actually backing up this kind of book with genuinely useful 'how to' information. There are definitely books in this category that redeem themselves by providing well-researched and very useful action to go with the inspiration.

✓ Getting media training and an image consultant to ensure you're ready to take on the 'pretty-boys', 'favourite-uncle' types, 'sciency-looking' people with funny accents and 'mumsy' super models.

Other Non-Fiction Book Archetypes

There are other archetypes such as memoirs, life stories, biographies, true crime and article compilations too but, as I said at the beginning of this book, I consider these books to be entertainment non-fiction at best and we're dealing with useful or utilitarian fiction – because it's easier to define a market and sell books like this.

Mapping Out Your Book

Our first business was website design and one of the first things we did with clients was to map out all the content using primary, secondary and tertiary levels. Of course some sites go much deeper than this but, for a book, I'd strongly urge you to stick to 3 levels maximum unless you like making your life (and that of your reader) difficult.

Here's how to map out your book visually so it's easy to plot progress and plan your writing...

1. Get a massive sheet of paper or (my favourite approach) loads of squares of scrap paper and a big table (so you can re-order stuff easily).

2. Map out your main 'big picture' topics and themes first. These will become your primary headings, chapters or sections. I tend to leave the essential elements such as foreword, acknowledgements, praise, introduction, about the author etc. out of this map because they should always be featured in a non-fiction book.

3. For each main topic add sub topics. These will be your secondary headings or sub-chapters. I like to write these as if I'm writing a headline for an article, which will come in handy when it comes to promoting your book anyway.

4. Optionally, for each sub topic, map out any tertiary topics. These are often just keywords to enable you to further split the subject down into manageable chunks for your audience.

You can see how the map for this book shaped up by viewing the Contents section – which shows all 3 levels.

Your Writing Voice

The style of writing can really make a big difference to the overall position of your book and the impact it has on you, your readers and your business. My personal style (I hope) is chatty, friendly, occasionally cheeky, but generally positive and encouraging. I know for a fact that this will work for some people and really annoy others but I'm not out to make *everyone* like me.

If you're planning to be seen as a serious authority then it may be best to take a more sober, balanced and less chatty approach but the cost could be a book that is harder to read (for some people) and a slower pace.

Some authors seem more comfortable telling long rambling stories that eventually get to a point while others tell you the punch line first and then fill in the detail. I prefer reading the latter but I'd argue that the former can be very effective too and will appeal to a different audience than me.

Your Core Voice

My advice is to write how you speak. This will ensure that your text is natural and congruent with the 'real you' should you find yourself on radio or TV or a YouTube video. However, some people are great actors and there's definitely a benefit in getting into a particular mindset (which may not be your usual private self) in order to make your book better. So, with that in mind, here are few voice characteristics to adpot or avoid...

Opinionated, Ranting, Cheeky, Jocular, Serious, Gravitas, Authoritative, Inclusive, Instructive, Supportive, Aggressive, Tough, Soft, Friendly, Energetic, Calm, Considered, Balanced, Nice, Self-Deprecating, Self-Confident etc.

Metaphorical or Literal

Sometimes a well chosen metaphor can say something far more elegantly than page after page of literal description. I'm a fan of metaphor because it's often more quotable, more interesting and more efficient than being literal. The easiest way to come up with metaphors is to think of an existing pattern, observation or problem and ask yourself, "what else is that like?"

Here's one I prepared earlier...

"Paying to get published is like paying for sex. No matter how you try to justify it you're still handing over cash to get screwed."

Joe Gregory, The Wealthy Author

Essentially, this is the simplest metaphor you can get but it makes it clear what I'm trying to get across in just a few words.

It's got a setup: "X is like Y"
And a punch line: "...because..."

Plus it's emotive because the comparison is so much more dramatic and undesirable than any amount of literal reasoning could be. Paying for sex isn't something most people would do and, even if they did, they're not likely to go bragging about it. So tying these two things together really spells out just how seedy and desperate it is to pay to get published.

This one line is infinitely more quotable than a whole chapter or the Comparison Matrices I share in Step 4.

The problem with metaphor though is that it distorts the facts by over-generalising and over-simplifying an issue. So, I'd use it sparingly, often as an attention grabbing device, and back it up with a more detailed and literal argument.

Why You Should Avoid Clichés Like The Plague

*"Be a first rate version of yourself, not
a second rate version of someone else."*

Judy Garland

Clichés are often difficult to avoid because they become part of
the normal way you speak. However, clichés are dangerous
because people simply ignore them or they've become so
commonplace they've lost any power to engage your reader.

There's nothing wrong with (or difficult about) playing with
existing clichés though to come up with something that makes the
reader stop, maybe smile and take notice of what you're saying.

Let's take the cliché I used jokingly for this heading, "Avoid This
Like The Plague" and see what fun we can have with a few
alternatives...

- ✓ "You should avoid clichés like a fat kid avoids salad"
- ✓ "You should avoid clichés like politicians avoid the truth"
- ✓ "You should avoid clichés like they're taxes"
- ✓ "You should avoid clichés" (this is still better than a cliché)

Make it your job when you review your work to look for clichés
and repurpose them like this or simply remove the cliché
completely! It's more quotable, marks your writing out as more
original and is a lot of fun!

Your Non-Fiction Book Blueprint

*"People don't care about you or your book.
They care about what it can do for them."*

Debbie Jenkins, www.leanmarketing.co.uk

The approach and outline we share on the following pages has
worked well for many of our other authors, and should enable
you to write your book in a paint-by-numbers way which means
you can get on with the job of writing (and sharing what you

know) and get it done quickly. This is just one way to do it though, so feel free to tweak the blueprint for your own needs...

INTRODUCTION

WHY SHOULD YOU READ THIS BOOK ANYWAY?

Make your big promise here, give anecdotes about other people who might be like your readers, including yourself. Prove the success you've had. Give figures and real examples where possible.

MY STORY

Really let them know you too were once where they are now. The story of your success will build credibility (so it's important that they know you're no longer 'that person') but a story about how you first failed, had doubts, struggled and yet succeeded against the odds makes a much more compelling read.

THE QUALIFYING SELF QUIZ?

A self quiz (Cosmo-style quiz) of 5-7 questions that defines exactly who you're writing for. Make it witty, but above all fill it with truisms for them, based on their pains/frustrations so you can begin matching their experience with your solution.

CHAPTER-BY-CHAPTER

Give a chapter by chapter commentary on what they'll be getting as a result of reading. If you can't make a compelling promise/headline for the chapter then rethink the purpose/direction of the chapter until you can.

HOW TO USE THIS BOOK

Not always necessary but if you plan to provide exercises/actions at the end of each chapter then tell them your preferred approach. Read the one at the beginning of this book for an example.

It's also important to have a consistent and (pretty much) identical structure for every single chapter in your book. Having the structure set in stone before you begin will really help keep things on target. Here's a suggested structure...

CHAPTER STRUCTURE

IN THIS CHAPTER...

Provide a bullet point list of the key topics/themes/ things you'll cover.

PACING STATEMENT

This is where you get them nodding as they're reading. Here's a quick example for a first chapter for a sales book...

If you're like most people, when you think of a salesman invariably an image of a slippery, grinning, conniving and thoroughly unsavoury type in a cheap suit, wearing too much aftershave and too much jewellery springs to mind. Well, it's little wonder... but as you'll soon discover the really good salespeople are nothing like this at all...

Of course, you'd change the heading here to something more specific than "PACING STATEMENT". If you've got statistics, figures, graphs or surveys that illustrate the reality then include them here instead or as well.

KEY POINT/LEADING 1, 2, 3 etc.

Each key point can also use the pacing-leading dynamic. Another quick example for a sales book...

"Being Pushy Doesn't Work" (which would be the title here)... When was the last time you enjoyed being harassed by an obviously desperate sales person? You know the type, fast-talking, pushy, not listening, running a script... The answer is probably never. So why do so many sales people think they have to be pushy? Do you remember the old fable about the wind and the sun?... Here are X reasons why listening and paying attention etc. is better...

SUMMARY

Tell them what you've just told them and what they should now know. It seems like a repeat of the opening "IN THIS CHAPTER..." which it virtually is but the tense will be different, ie in the past which reinforces the key points. I'd also write a sentence or two setting them up (opening loops) for the next chapter or your exercise...

EXERCISE

This is optional but if you choose to do it you should have an exercise for *every* main chapter in the book. Keep it simple and get them applying your points in the real world as quickly as possible.

AFTERWORD

This isn't necessary but a simple chapter that reminds people of your key points, brings things all together and leads them to take action and use what they've learned is always a nice way to finish off a book and not leave them hanging.

Style Rules: Consistency & Standards

This short checklist is based on our own brief for editors. You may want to make your own rules but this will at least point you at some of the things you need to make consistent. I suggest you become familiar with Hart's Rules which can be found in the *Oxford Guide To Style* or if you're using International (US) English you can read *The Chicago Manual of Style.*

- ✓ **Consistency** – spellings, hyphens, punctuation, formatting and spacing should be applied consistently throughout the document.

- ✓ **Table of contents** to be included – use Microsoft's Word's built in tool.

- ✓ **Chapter headings** numbered 1, 2, 3 etc. Not Chapter One just 1 where needed.

- ✓ **Sub-headings** made compelling (like a headline) or instructive (clear what's included) as appropriate. Be consistent.

- ✓ **Chapter structure** is consistent with each chapter having same sub sections e.g. Intro, Examples, Summary etc. for every chapter.

- ✓ **Format heading levels** using Heading 1, Heading 2, Heading 3 etc.

- ✓ **Format body text** as 'Normal' and use only italics and bold as appropriate for emphasis.

- ✓ **Capitals** – do not use for stress only use for acronyms and to begin the title of people or things. To stress a word in a sentence use italics not capitals.

- ✓ **Italics** is only for foreign words, stress and titles of books etc.

- ✓ **Bold** can also be used for stress especially to introduce points in bullet lists as used here. Do not use bold to indicate a sub-heading.

- ✓ **Hyphens** – use sparingly but almost always use for words that begin with anti, non and neo and to avoid ambiguities e.g. "a little-used car" versus "a little used-car".

- ✓ **Leader dots** – are a special typographic character and should consist of just 3 dots and no more – ... is acceptable .... is not.

- ✓ **Exclamations and Questions** – only ever use one punctuation point e.g. ! not !!! – ? not ??? – Do not mix - ?!? is unacceptable.

- ✓ **New paragraphs** should be separated by a line break fully left aligned with no indent.

- ✓ **New sentences** should have single spaces (not double or triple) after punctuation for previous sentence.

- ✓ **Speech** – begin with double inverted commas e.g. "The publisher told me, 'always use double inverted commas first for our titles,' so I do."

✓ **Jargon, acronyms, abbreviations** – explain/define any jargon word or acronym when it's first used and use shortcut afterwards. Don't put full stops in an acronym e.g. use NATO not N.A.T.O.

✓ **Short Words** should be used in place of long ones where sensible because they are easy to spell and easy to understand. In general we prefer: about to approximately – after to following – let to permit – but to however – use to utilise – make to manufacture – take part to participate – set up to establish – enough to sufficient – show to demonstrate – help to assistance – find out to ascertain etc.

✓ **Fluff Words** should be removed where practical. See how it reads if you shorten words e.g. track record to record – weather conditions to weather – large-scale to large – this time around to this time – free of charge to free – safe haven to haven – most probably to probably etc.

✓ **Very** – if this word occurs in a sentence then try removing it to see if the meaning is changed. "The omens are good" may be more powerful than "The omens are very good". Never use "very, very".

✓ **Spelling** – use British English – ise/isation not ize/ization – labour not labor – colour not color. Also use while not whilst – amid not amidst etc.

✓ **Active voice** is preferred over the passive voiced. "The book was written" is better as "She wrote the book".

✓ **Sentences** should be short and punchy not long and meandering. Simplify long expressions where possible e.g. "now" is better than "at this moment in time" – "if" is better than "In the event that" etc.

✓ **Dates** – use dd-mm-yyyy or, to avoid ambiguity entirely, Day Month Year.

Know Your Daily & Hourly Word Count Targets

"How do you move a mountain?
One stone at a time!"

A 40,000 word manuscript can seem daunting if it's not tackled correctly so it's important to break it down into manageable chunks and to ensure your deadline is realistic. Here's how:

1. Map out your book so that you know how many chapters it will contain and all the chunks of information you require.
2. Know your target word count.
3. Know your deadline.
4. Work backwards from your deadline and count how many writing days you have available (don't forget to allow for breaks).
5. This should give you a rough daily word count target.
6. Now divide this figure by the number of productive hours you can write in a day – I'd base it on 5 hours – to get your hourly word count target.
7. Is this target realistic, achievable or possible? If not you may need to re-adjust your deadline or if the deadline is immovable you're going to have to put in longer days until the hourly word count figure is manageable.

Immunising Yourself Against Writer's Block

Blocks can happen for all kinds of reasons and if you happen to be really struggling with this a lot then I highly recommend Tom Evans' excellent book on the subject (which we're proud to have published) entitled *Blocks.*

However, there are plenty of things you can do from the outset of your writing project *and* as you progress to minimise the risk and almost block-proof yourself.

✓ **Do things in the correct order.** If you recall what I said earlier in the part on creativity then you'll know that it's difficult (if not impossible) to try to create ideas at the same time as editing them – it's the equivalent of speaking while attempting to listen. Well the same applies to writing too. So remember to do the right things at the right time... Plan/Map Out, Create, Review and Improve as distinct and separate steps.

✓ **Create a vacuum that needs to be filled.** The process of mapping out your book and then including all the empty headings for each chapter is a deliberate way to create a vacuum that you'll feel compelled to fill with new content. So don't miss these important steps or you could end up getting bogged down.

✓ **Clear your calculator.** This is based on Maxwell Maltz's advice in the excellent book Psycho-Cybernetics (a book I recommend you read if you're interested in how to improve your built in goal-seeking and success-seeking abilities). Basically if you've got other stuff on your mind while you're trying to write your book then you'll be trying to do two things at once. Write all your other thoughts down onto a Do Later list or if you have an urgent and important job that's playing on your mind then get it done first.

✓ **Plan breaks into your writing schedule.** This is all about personal style. I prefer to write in big spurts of 3-4 hours non-stop with an hour to recover. Others prefer to do it in short sharp blasts of 45 minutes on and 15 off. Experiment until you find the optimal approach for you.

✓ **Go on an information diet.** This is related to clearing your calculator but if your book required a research phase you should have done this before starting writing. I highly recommend not watching or reading the news, reading any other books (even fiction) or using any instructional videos/audios while you're writing because once you're in a generative state your mind will automatically try to create connections with everything, which is not always useful as your ideas begin to evolve due to new information.

Step 4: Getting Your Book Published

"Paying to get published is like paying for sex. No matter how you try to justify it, you're still handing over cash to get screwed."

Joe Gregory, The Wealthy Author

So many first time authors have stumbled here and all their hard work simply sits gathering dust. But, much to the chagrin of many 'traditionally' published authors, there's no longer a barrier to getting your book in print and selling via the same channels as the big publishers. But just because the barriers are down it doesn't necessarily mean the road is easy.

The good news is that by the time you've finished this chapter you'll know exactly how to get published and you won't fall prey to the many scammers out there who unashamedly try to cash in on other people's dreams.

Comparison: Do It Yourself, Win A Publishing Contract or Pay A Vanity Press?

I've included vanity presses in this matrix for completeness but as the purpose of this book is to help you become a *wealthy* author I'd suggest you avoid all fee-based publishers completely because (no matter what they say) their business model is based on selling you *their services* and *not* on selling your books (except to you)!

Also, not all mainstream publishers are equal. Some, like our own company, offer better terms, higher royalties and are less risk averse but are small by comparison to the big conglomerates so don't have the same level of kudos. While others will pay you a pittance but the kudos of being published by them is sometimes worth the price.

Finally, I strongly recommend that you use Print On Demand (POD) production processes for your first (and at least the following 49) self-publishing projects. I'll explain more about why later.

Your Publishing Options... At-A-Glance	SELF - POD	SELF - OLD	MAINSTREAM	VANITY
Guaranteed ALL of the profit from sales of your book	●	●		
Guaranteed LOTS of the profit from sales of your book				●
Guaranteed SOME of the profit from sales of your book			●	
Keep ALL intellectual rights to your work	●	●		
Keep MANY intellectual rights to your work				●
Keep FEW (if any) intellectual rights to your work			●	
Somebody else pays for and manages all design/production			●	
Somebody else buys, manages and owns ISBN number			●	●
Somebody else pays for initial print run			●	
Somebody else warehouses and/or ships your book	●		●	●
Somebody else handles distribution of your book	●		●	●
Most of the financial risk is taken by somebody else			●	
Kudos of being published by a "proper" publisher			●	
Stigma of paying a "vanity press" to publish your book				●
May get paid an advance (though less and less likely today)			●	
Everything (except the writing) gets done for you by experts			●	
Author copies of your book available to buy "at print cost"	●	●		
Book almost always designed/produced to a professional standard			●	
You don't need a publisher to say yes to get "in print"	●	●		●
Book instantly available to most major book retailers	●		●	●
Book is likely to be stocked by most bricks and mortar retailers			●	
Book is likely to be sold by Amazon and other online bookstores	●		●	●
Somebody else does ALL the marketing for you	N	O	P	E
Somebody else does SOME of the marketing for you			●	
Very likely to get your book to market in less than 12 months	●	●		●

Pros & Cons of Landing A Mainstream Publisher

*"When everyone thinks alike,
'everyone' is likely to be wrong."*

Humphrey Neill, The Art of Contrary Thinking

Although this is often the dream for many aspiring authors, landing a publishing contract with a mainstream publisher is not for everyone. In fact, if you're planning to be a *wealthy* author – especially with non-fiction – then I'd suggest that doing it yourself could be far more lucrative. But before we get ahead of ourselves let's look at some facts...

Being Published By A Mainstream Isn't Always So Great

✗ Many authors never actually earn their advance back – in other words the only money they'll ever see is the advance – and for the hours involved – they could have earned more by flipping burgers!

✗ Typical royalties for most non-fiction authors is 6%-8% net. About 50p per book sold for an averagely priced title.

✗ The people who make any real money from mainstream publishing are booksellers and publishing giants. Yet many of these companies are now struggling to survive as recent advances further level the playing field.

✗ A huge proportion of books 'sold' to book sellers by large publishers are returned unsold or sold off as 'remainders'. Sales of these books (because they're classed as salvage) provide ZERO income for the author in most cases.

✗ Mainstream publishers typically give a book 3 months in bookstores before giving up all hope of making further sales. If the book doesn't perform well they just abandon the marketing/distribution to focus on new titles.

7 Reasons Why You Do Want A 'Proper' Publishing Contract

1. **Kudos:** This is the biggy. If you simply want to brag that you've been published by a 'proper' publishing house and you know this can translate into a higher media profile, higher fees and a shot at fame then go for it!

2. **Distribution:** Your book (at least for a limited time) is likely to find its way onto more bookstore's shelves than if you were to self-publish. Although being on a shelf in a bookshop amongst loads of other books is no guarantee of success (especially as more and more sales are going online) it is likely you will make more actual sales (not necessarily profit) than if you were to self-publish.

3. **Focus:** Lots of the jobs you do as a self-publisher will take your focus away from your main job of writing. So, if you plan to spend most of your day writing books and not handling all manner of admin tasks then a publishing deal works well for you.

4. **Risk Aversion:** If you're completely risk averse or just plain broke then landing a contract with a proper publisher means you won't have to fork out anything for the production of your book. They'll do it all for you and, if you're lucky (or famous or very cool), they may even give you an advance. This means other than the time you spend writing (that could have otherwise been spent doing a real job that pays you for your time) you don't need any funds to get started.

5. **Fiction:** If you're writing fiction then I would strongly suggest that you try to get an agent and mainstream publishing contract before considering self-publishing. Even though you'll get paid less profit than a self-published author you'll really struggle to compete on price (it's typically lower for fiction than non-fiction) if you decided to self-publish. Plus, it's much harder to gain a platform for fiction than non-fiction if you don't have a 'proper' publisher with links to literary reviewers. Seriously, your odds are not good if you want to go it alone in fiction.

7 Reasons Why You Don't Want A 'Proper' Publishing Contract

1. **Loss of Freedom:** When you work for a publisher (because that's what you'll really be doing) much of your creative freedom (and your freedom of speech) will be quelled. They'll want to ensure your book fits their brand and they'll have their own (often good though sometimes not) ideas about how the book should look, what it will be called and what you're allowed to say.

2. **Loss of Control:** What you can do with your book (or even say about your book) will be severely limited. You may need to get approval for a marketing or advertising campaign you'd like to run and your ability to write another book with another publisher (or even to self-publish) may be subject to certain conditions in your contract. So, you may think you're only signing over rights to *one book* but you could end up signing over your creative soul too!

3. **Loss of Ownership:** Many large publishers will stipulate that they own the rights to your work in other languages, territories and formats. Be careful what you're signing and ensure you know your rights. Otherwise you could end up watching your publisher get rich while you remain penniless.

4. **Lack of Marketing**: Once the average mainstream publisher organises distribution and sticks your book in their catalogue forget about it! I'll keep saying this but, as an author, promotion is 100% your job! Even if you're a big name celebrity or you have just come off the back of a best-seller (which you will have had to work hard to promote) your publisher still won't be able to do the interviews for you. You have to be the spokesperson for your book and that means you're going to need to hustle!

5. **Loss of Profit:** I've already mentioned that you'll be paid the 'mouse's share' of the proceeds from your book sales but it gets worse if you have to use an agent too. You may have to give even more of your profit (and soul) away to agents in order to find a mainstream publisher. Some publishers – especially fiction – won't even deal directly with authors without an agent. Don't get me wrong,

some agents are fantastic people who'll protect the author's best interests, work proactively on your behalf and really do earn their keep. However, trying to land a good agent can be just as difficult as landing a publishing deal, and all the time you're trying to find an agent, you won't be making a penny from your big idea!

6. **Loss of Time & Opportunity:** You could spend more money and time chasing a publishing contract or agent than you could if you just got on with it and self-published. And if you consider that until you sell books the whole process is still a 'cost-money' exercise you don't want to be hanging around.

7. **Lack of Speed:** Publishing behemoths are full of really talented people, but they're also slow, cumbersome and full of political, financial and shareholder pressures. This all leads to a long delay between landing a deal and selling any books (if you don't even get an advance it's just not a good plan).

The Real Cost of Their 'Impressive' Distribution

Many fans of traditional publishers will cite improved distribution as a main reason to give up all your rights and most of your profits, but this distribution comes at a considerable cost – which you – as the author bear the brunt of.

Traditional publishers get onto bookstore's shelves by offering ridiculous terms (inflated discounts and return/destroy policies), paying them bribes (as much as £50,000 during Christmas) and paying the author just a little more than nothing in royalties.

But just because the spine of your book appears on a bookshop's shelf it doesn't mean you'll sell any more books. In fact, it's often more of an ego trip for the author to see their book in a 'proper' bookshop, than a viable route to market.

Just ask any publisher or veteran author what they hate most about the publishing business and they'll say the same thing: what they hate most is returns - because they get a lot of them. In fact (if they got lots of distribution but the book didn't sell anyway) it's often cheaper for them to let the bookshop destroy the books (or 'dispose' of them as remainders) than it is to take them back.

Plus, the current deal between bookstores and publishers is an out-dated waste-intensive – trees, time and profit – model which guarantees authors get paid a pittance in royalties. When all the waste is taken into account there's not much profit left for authors.

It Makes Financial Sense To Self-Publish... Even If You Do It Badly

"Always have a reason why you're doing something. If you don't have one – don't do it."

Debbie Jenkins, www.leanmarketing.co.uk

Many self-publishers (who self-published because they worked out the profit they could make rather than doing it as a last resort) would not want a mainstream book deal because the pay (even with a highly successful title) sucks.

In fact, even a complete publishing newbie with awful distribution can still make loads more money by self publishing than by going mainstream.

To give you an idea of how a typical mainstream book deal could really be a bad idea (if your goal is to make money and not simply to get into bookshops) here's a real (figures rounded up for simplicity) example of our own first self-published book, *The Gorillas Want Bananas*. Here are the numbers from our first self-published book:

- ✓ We printed 3,000 copies of *The Gorillas Want Bananas* (this was before POD) which cost approx £3,500. We had no distribution except direct sales (speaking gigs, training seminars and our website) and Amazon (though we're talking about Amazon Advantage here which isn't the same as a proper listing).

✓ We sold out of this first print run within 18 months. The book sold for an average of £15 per sale (after discounts, the RRP was £25 back then) so minus costs and postage this translated to roughly £10 profit per book. Plus 70% of buyers became leads on our database (which if you have backend products you'll realise is more valuable than the initial sales anyway).

✓ We did a second print run of 3,000 (with lower costs because the plates were already made) and sold out of those too. Selling for roughly £12 per book, for approx £8 profit per book.

Approx Total setup costs (not including postage): £5,500
Approx Total revenue: £54,000
Approx Total profit (after costs): £48,500

Now, let's assume a mainstream publisher would have brought us 5 times more sales (though I very much doubt it based on how much we hustled to sell what we did)...

✗ They would have set the cover price to £12.99 max.

✗ Assume 7% royalties (net) after costs/discounts and they discount at 65% (typical) leaving approx £4.55 profit per book. 7% of that for the author is almost 32p per book - wow!

✗ Now assuming 5 times more sales due to better distribution (though many mainstreams state that a non-fiction book is successful if it sells more than 2,000 copies) we would have sold 30,000 books (and had no way to get any of those buyers easily onto our database).

✗ 30,000 x 32p = £9,600! So we'd have been £38,900 worse off even if we sold 5 times more books by using a traditional mainstream publisher - no thanks!

In fact, even if a mainstream had sold *20 times* more books (120,000 compared to our measly 6,000)... that would still only be £38,400 for us. It just wouldn't have made financial sense. Plus, most publishers - despite having distribution - don't do any serious promotion on their author's behalf so we'd have been stupid to go the mainstream route.

Why A Publisher Is Against Mainstream Publishing

In case you're wondering why we're knocking mainstream publishing, even though we run a publishing company ourselves, then consider this. We run a publishing business that is now able to get the same distribution as our bigger rivals (it took us 50 books to get past the initial block) but here's where we differ...

- ✓ We call the shots (the bookshops don't).
- ✓ We only do firm sale (no returns).
- ✓ We only offer 35% discount (not 65% and up).
- ✓ We believe in paying the author more than we pay the bookshop (our royalties go as high as 50%).
- ✓ Our terms make most traditional bookshops unwilling to stock our book but we don't care because...
- ✓ We create demand with buyers so the bookshop has to either stock it (which they do for some of our books) or lose the sale to online stores.

So, by setting the author up as the king/queen (and paying upto 40% - and 50% in special cases - royalties) we've turned things on their head. Do the numbers based on our deal (it starts at 20%) and if it looks appealing then get in touch at *www.bookshaker.com/authors*

Getting Published By A Mainstream Publisher

Right, now that I've shared the pros and cons of being published by a mainstream publisher you're in a better position to decide if this route is right for you. And, if it is, we'll do all we can to help you find a publisher for you and your book.

If this is the route for you then I recommend you buy and read *Get Your Book Published* by, the prolifically published, Susan St Maur which covers all kinds of things like handling reviewer's feedback, checking out the contract and ensuring you create a compelling pitch.

12 Steps To Landing A Publishing Contract

1. Make sure you've read Step 1 and 2 in this book and that you have a good idea with commercial potential first.

2. Once you know you have a bestselling idea, killer title and market of hungry fanatics then make a list of your goals.

3. If you're after profits and income over fame and kudos then stop now and consider self-publishing instead.

4. If you'd prefer reach, fame and kudos and you're willing to give away the lion's share of the profit (and jump through a few hoops) for this then keep reading.

5. Shortlist publishers you'd like to work with. For non-fiction I'd seriously suggest you go direct to the publisher if you can (even if they say they only accept submissions from agents it's worth sending a quick email or letter to check) For a great list of publishers buy *The Writer's And Artist's Yearbook* (*www.writersandartists.co.uk*) or take a look at the resources at *www.publishingacademy.com*

6. Don't send unsolicited manuscripts, especially if the publisher explicitly says not to. They'll likely destroy it unopened and ignore you in future. Publishers don't do this to be mean but to protect themselves from law suits from snubbed authors who might believe their great idea (which wasn't) got stolen and used. If they never saw it and never read it they've got a great defence.

7. If a publisher really requires you to approach them via an agent then I'd personally look for a different publisher first or ask them to refer you to agents they recommend (see the next list on getting an agent).

8. Find out what a publisher's submission guidelines are and follow these to the letter to present your detailed synopsis but ignore their rules about not chasing up (as long as you do it in a friendly and assertive way). Still, you should give them plenty of time (because they're often slow and have to deal with loads of enquiries just like yours). If you can't stand the long time delays between pitching and getting a rejection (or acceptance) then consider publishing your book yourself – it doesn't get any faster!

9. Ignore the old politics of only offering your book to one publisher at a time (and waiting obediently for them to reject it) unless you like waiting for a year between pitches and you're not afraid of starving to death in the meantime. Instead choose your top 5 publishers and send your synopsis to all of them. Then if you end up in the fortunate position to have two or more publishers interested you can play them off against each other!

10. Don't tell a traditional mainstream publisher that you've already written your book. Even though you'd think this would put you ahead of someone who simply has a 'good idea' you'd be wrong – so keep quiet unless the publisher in question explicitly states that they accept complete manuscripts. Why? Because many publishers will reject your book as soon as they know you've already written it. Why? Because they've always done it like that and traditional publishers like to maintain tradition. Why? Because at one time they used to add value by planning the book with their author but these days they rarely have the budget or resources. Just for the record – *www.bookshaker.com* accepts (and gives priority to) completed manuscripts.

11. Never forget that the publisher really does have what you want so the balance of power lies with them. There are only so many publishers around offering what you want and need but by contrast there are thousands of authors and writers with books looking to work with them. In other words, if you don't like the game choose a new one (like self-publishing) but throwing a tantrum won't ingratiate you to publishers so don't waste your time.

12. Have realistic expectations. Forget the days of huge advances and be happy if you get any advance at all. Expect 7% net in royalties as the norm and don't expect them to move from this position unless you're willing to give something else up. Don't expect much (if anything) in the way of marketing support. If they want to pay you a one-off fee but no ongoing royalties then you won't get wealthy this way – reconsider your options.

What Publishers Are Really Looking For

Your book and big idea is really just one (often undervalued) element of the package publishers are looking for from authors today.

No matter how great your idea is a good publisher will be looking beyond the book at the bigger picture. This will include you (as the author and main marketer), your attitude (and ability to take orders without becoming a pain), your platform (how many fans ie prospective buyers you have), how good your marketing plan (a synopsis should really be a marketing/business plan with a book bolted on the front) is and how credible you seem to be.

The Author's Marketing Platform

The old saying that it's not what you know but who you know almost rings true here. Almost, the following is probably closer though...

> *"It's not about what you know or even who you know but about who knows you."*
>
> Debbie Jenkins, www.leanmarketing.co.uk

More and more publishers can afford to be picky and they'll want to see that you're bringing more than a book and a big idea to the party. Publishers today expect authors to come to them with a ready-made platform of ready-primed prospects and fans.

This means a mailing list of people interested in your book, a big social network (Twitter, Facebook, MySpace, YouTube, LinkedIn etc.) and an impressive Google/Media footprint (basically how much visibility you already have) where it counts. All of these things will need to be built as part of your book marketing campaign anyway but be sure to spell out how you, the author, are a hot property in your proposal and if you're not then consider ways you can make up for this (say with a killer marketing plan) or by self-publishing first and building a list at the same time.

The Author's Marketing Savvy

I know I keep repeating this but I'll continue to repeat it because it's really important...

"You, and only you, are ultimately responsible for selling your book."

With this in mind you need to display your willingness and ability to promote yourself and your book effectively to prospective publishers.

The one-sheet (see next chapter) is a good opportunity to show off your persuasive powers but there's more to it than that and you should make it your job, as a budding wealthy author, to learn what you can about self-promotion and marketing your expertise.

It's really not that difficult and there are now more opportunities than ever to raise your profile with a very small budget. So, as well as reading Step 5 of this book I also recommend you add these books to your library, and more importantly, read them...

Influence by Robert Cialdini, *The 22 Immutable Laws of Marketing* by Al Ries & Jack Trout, *The Gorillas Want Bananas* by Debbie Jenkins & yours truly, *Selling The Invisible* by Harry Beckwith, *MediaMasters* by Jeremy Nicholas & Alan Stevens, *Bare Knuckle Selling* by Simon Hazeldine and *Persuasion Skills Black Book* by Rintu Basu. You'll be a whole lot further ahead!

The Author's Personality

In our business we have a very simple rule of thumb for spotting an author we'd like to work with. We want to know if they're going to be 'resource-full' or 'resource-needy'. Which are you?

Resource-full authors...

✓ Demonstrate successes by pointing out things they have already achieved.

✓ Will have left a trail a publisher can follow quite easily by looking at their website, doing a quick Google search on them, reading their blog etc.

✓ Will respond to criticism positively and with solutions and suggestions for improvement.

✓ Will ask good questions that relate to measurable outcomes, especially where book sales and marketing is concerned.

✓ Will be excited about the marketing and writing challenge ahead of them.

Resource-needy authors...

✗ Talk about things they want to achieve – with little evidence of past success.

✗ May say they've achieved a lot but have no real online or media trail to prove it.

✗ Will respond to criticism negatively or ask for too much feedback before doing anything.

✗ Will want to know what the publisher is going to do for them.

✗ Will be daunted by the marketing or openly say they're not into marketing.

Of course, authors can easily act as if they're resource-full but as checking up on them using Google becomes easier it's not all that hard for a publisher to call their bluff.

Do You Have A Face For Radio?

"What someone else thinks of me is none of my bloody business!"

Debbie Jenkins, www.leanmarketing.co.uk

Many publishers will also have biases that have nothing to do with your book, your skills or your marketing acumen.

They'll want to see how 'media friendly' you are, in other words, "mingers need not apply" because if all else is equal then a good looking, young and smiley model-type is more likely to get the TV gig (and promotional exposure) than a normal looking old geezer with bad teeth. I'm not saying it's fair (or that they'll freely admit it) but 'how you look' can make a difference with more and more publishers looking for reasons to say no.

So, if you are funny looking or you're no spring chicken then make sure you use this fact to your advantage and consider overplaying your weaknesses in order to turn them into a strength.

Self Test: Are You Hot or Not?

Score yourself on the following statements as follows: 0 = disagree totally, 1 = agree slightly, 2 = agree totally

☐ I have thousands of hungry fans eagerly waiting for the arrival of my book.

☐ I understand my role in the marketing of my book and have I prepared adequately for it.

☐ I am able to follow plans and take action quickly.

☐ I have prepared myself for media opportunities.

☐ I have been building a relationship with useful contacts and preparing them for the arrival my book.

☐ I have a wide-reaching and keyword-relevant web presence across multiple platforms.

☐ I have demonstrated my expertise (not just talked about it).

YOUR SCORE

0-5: Freezing! Don't waste your time contacting publishers until you understand what they're really looking for. A great idea for a book won't get published unless the author has what it takes to promote, market and hustle.

5-10: Decidedly cool! Getting there, but still lots of room for improvement. Look at using the internet to create a raving fan base; it's cheap, measurable and fun. Start out with Facebook to get you started. Then look at LinkedIn for building excellent contacts.

10+: Hot Stuff! You know what publishers want – a great book idea, backed up by a hot author! If you scored this highly we may want to publish you so get in touch at *www.bookshaker.com/authors* if you'd like to work with us.

Essential Stuff You'll Need To Get Published

A Riveting One-Sheet

Your one-sheet should be riveting, exciting and interesting while making it clear where the market is. In some ways this little page is responsible for 80% of the final decision so make it count. You will usually send it as part of your initial enquiry. Its job is essentially to get the publisher to request a full proposal.

Here's a sample one-sheet taken from *Get Your Book Published* by Susan St Maur for her book *Powerwriting* (published by Prentice Hall in 2002) to give you an idea what's involved...

"Powerwriting: The hidden skills you need to transform your business writing" by Suzan St Maur

In our high-tech age, the written word in business is even more powerful than ever before. Yet millions are wasted every year on business communications that don't work. In 90% of cases, such failure has little to do with the quality of writing (or design/ production.) It's due to a lack of understanding of the audience, and the message being conveyed in the wrong way - in other words, inappropriate and inadequate thought. Powerwriting is the first book of its kind to teach you the thought processes you need to work through before you even put pen to paper or fingers to keyboard. Then it shows you how to use those thought processes to harness the power of words for business and other communications that get powerful results every time.

This fresh new business book will provide invaluable help to the rapidly increasing number of business people and other individuals who write their own business communications. The arrival of the internet has consolidated what already was a growing trend away from the use of professional communicators. Most people in business or other activities are now on their own, other than for "above-the-line" advertising. Marketing and other training courses merely skim the surface of business writing, and existing books and courses focus largely on the crafting of words rather than the thinking behind them, which often leads to catastrophic results - see above.

Powerwriting, therefore, is targeted at anyone aiming to influence readers or viewers through their writing, online or offline, whether they're in a small or large business, government department, charity, political party, hobby/special interest group or any other area of activity.

Non-parochial, Powerwriting is suitable for all English-language markets and is also suitable for translation into other major languages as well as online/audio publication. Its style is informal, personal, and humorous in places. In effect, it is a "sharing" of valuable experience and true common sense between author and reader.

Its author, Canadian-born Suzan St Maur, has a long and successful track record both as an author (6 published books including 3 previous business communications titles) and as one of the UK's leading business communications writers over the last 20 years.

Anticipated length is 60,000 - 80,000 words. Delivery time 6-10 months from signing of contract. Full proposal, detailed chapter synopses and sample chapter available on request.

A Sample of Your Best Bits

Publishers' requirements vary here, some will want to see a table of contents and a single chapter (to see how you write) while others may ask you to write a specific chapter after seeing only the table of contents while providing a brief (to test your order taking ability too). Yet others will expect a good sample, say 5 chapters.

I'd personally plan to write 3-5 chapters of your book (the stuff that really opens loops, makes big promises and whets the reader's appetite) and have it ready for when a publisher asks to see it. You'll almost always have to format this differently for different publishers so follow their guidelines or ask for their guidelines if you can't find any.

Your Non-Fiction Book Proposal & Synopsis

You'll often need to rework this to fit an individual publisher's requirements. But your basic synopsis should answer the following questions (once you've worked through the other sections of this book you should be able to answer these questions easily and confidently)...

- ✓ **Competition:** What other books on the subject exist and why is yours better than the rest?
- ✓ **Market/Audience:** Who will want the book and why will it appeal to them? Why do you think the topic of your book is hot right now? What evidence do you have? What's the anticipated market size?
- ✓ **Big Promise/Big Idea:** What's the big promise or your big idea? Is your book contentious or groundbreaking in some way? What's your book's "wow factor"?
- ✓ **Impact:** What will your book do for the reader and how will they behave, think or feel differently? How will things be better for them after reading your book?
- ✓ **Style:** Is your book informal or formal? Academic or experiential? Practical or theoretical? How-to or inspirational? Will it shock? Will it inform? Will it in encourage and inspire?
- ✓ **Endorsements:** Could you get a suitable famous person or big name to write a foreword? Do you have any praise or fans already?
- ✓ **Author:** Why are you uniquely positioned to write (and more importantly) promote this book? What other books have you written? What are your credentials?

In addition to answering these questions with your synopsis your detailed proposal should include:

- ✓ **Delivery information:** anticipated word count (you should find out how many words they usually publish and go for that), anticipated time required to complete etc.
- ✓ **Chapter list:** preferably with a title and as many bullet pointed details as possible for each one, write these as if they're article headlines for added impact.
- ✓ **Sample chapter or excerpts:** 1,000 words or so to demonstrate style and approach, these should be your best bits (as already detailed).
- ✓ **Your Platform:** Do you already have a fan base? How many people are on your mailing list? How many visitors does your blog get? How many people make up your

online social network? What other platforms, groups and clubs do you belong to or run?

✓ **Your Marketing Plan:** How do you intend to reach your target audience? Are you planning to invest your own time and money into marketing your book? Will you be writing and giving away articles? Do you have a good media list? What specific marketing skills do you bring? Will you be doing public speaking? Are you planning to buy lots of books to sell direct? Are you prepared to take full responsibility for marketing? (In case you haven't worked it out, the publisher would like your answer to be yes to most, if not all of these!)

Detailed examples of real proposals (ones that were successful for us and other authors) are available to members of our Publishing Academy. Go to *www.publishingacademy.com* now to take a look.

The Commissioning Editor's Job Is To Say No

"Try saying no to everything for a whole week."

Joe Gregory, www.leanmarketing.co.uk

The commissioning editor (or agent) will be looking for any reason at all to reject your proposal. While this is a bit simplistic and cynical it happens to be true. If you think about it publishers simply have to take short cuts in order to wade through the huge numbers of book ideas they get sent every day.

Here's how it typically goes with a big mainstream publisher…

How To Fail Before Your Book Gets Looked At

✗ Fail to follow their "no unsolicited manuscript" policy - No

✗ Fail to send it in the type of envelope they specified – No

✗ Fail to format your synopsis exactly as they specified – No

✗ Fail to include all the answers they expected – No

How To Fail As Soon As They Look At Your Proposal

- ✗ Give inadequate answers to key questions – No

- ✗ Say your book is for "anybody and everybody" – No

- ✗ Say your manuscript is already complete – No

- ✗ Come across like a prima donna in any way – No

- ✗ Forget to mention marketing information - No

- ✗ Lead them to believe in any way that you expect them to do the marketing while you pick up the royalties from a beach in the Caribbean - No

How To Fail Even When They're Interested

- ✗ Negotiate too aggressively over the contract – No

- ✗ Tell them you need to think about it – No

- ✗ Moan about the deadline they set – No

- ✗ Start making demands about the title, content etc. – No

So now you know their game you'll realise that your job isn't so much about convincing them to say 'yes' but avoiding all the pitfalls that could get your book dumped before you even get a chance. Remember, find out what they want and give it to them or you'll waste more time than you need to.

Independent Publishers

So far we've discussed mainstream publishers which, for the purpose of this book, are pretty large, well-established organisations that hold a lot of power and probably belong to a handful of much larger conglomerates.

However, the terms, approaches and flexibility of independent publishers is far more varied and they're likely to offer you a better contract, more control and higher royalties – while getting good if not *as good* distribution and cost-savings.

What they rarely give however, is the same level of credibility of their bigger rivals. But I'd say this isn't worth as much as most people think anyway.

Our own little Independent publishing firm (*www.bookshaker.com*) is a member of the IPG (Independent Publishers Guild) in the UK so if you're looking for a publishing contract and like the idea of working with an independent then get in touch with them for a list of members (or advice) *www.ipg.uk.com*

Or if you're in the USA then try The Independent Book Publisher's Association (formerly PMA) at *www.pma-online.org* and SPAN (The Small Publishers Association of North America) at *www.spannet.org*

Independent publisher will often ask similar questions to the mainstreams but are almost certainly faster at responding and more likely to take a risk on an unknown author or first-timer.

Comparison: Vanity (Fee-Based) Publishers

If, despite all my warnings, you'd still prefer to pay someone to take the hassle (and your money) off you then it's worth knowing your options. If you have a good *non-fiction* book idea though then please do anything but go with a vanity press. The only exceptions are if you want your poetry or fiction in print and you're absolutely certain you're not going to get a proper publishing deal otherwise and you don't want the hassle of doing proper self-publishing.

Please note: the following comparison is independent and has been compiled based on the best available data. If you feel we've misrepresented one of these providers then please contact us and we'll update the book immediately as well as post an addendum at *www.publishingacademy.com*

Fee-Based Publishers (aka Vanity Publishers) At-A-Glance	OUTSKIRTS PRESS	BOOKLOCKER	ECADEMY PRESS	TRAFFORD	XLIBRIS	AUTHORHOUSE	iUNIVERSE
Price of Cheapest Package (USD $) * indicates approx price based on exchange rate	199	299	1,615 *	799	299	598	599
Advertised Time From Manuscript To Market (weeks)	-	4	12	12	12	12	12
Standard Royalty Paid To Author % (Retail Sales)	-	15	20	20	10	10	20
Use LightningSource for Print and Distribution	●	●	●	●	●	●	●
Number of "Free" Author Copies Provided	1	0	10	0	0	5	5
Author Copies Price Based on Discount Off Cover Price	●		●	●	●	●	●
Author Copies Price Based on Actual Print Costs		●					
Amazon Distribution - Variable Availability (Included)		●	●	●		●	●
Amazon Distribution - Variable Availability (Extra)	●				●		
Distribution To Offline Bookstores (Included)		●	●	●		●	●
Basic Proofing Included				●			●
Distribution To Offline Bookstores (Extra)	●				●		
Cover Design or Template (Included)	●		●	●	●	●	●
Cover Design or Template (Extra)		●					
Will Indicate Your Books As Published By Them	●	●	●	●	●	●	●
Will Put Their Logo On Your Book			●	●	●	●	●
Assignment of ISBN (Included)			●	●	●	●	●
Assignment of ISBN (Extra)	●						
They Keep Ownership of ISBN	●		●	●	●	●	
Allow You To Use Your Own ISBN At No Extra Cost		●					
Hidden Charges (Photos etc.)	●			●	●	●	●
Charge Extra to produce/provide a PDF of Your Book	●			●	●	●	●
Marketing Services Available At Extra Cost	●		●	●	●	●	●

Trafford, Xlibris, AuthorHouse and iUniverse are all owned by the same parent company.

Vanity Presses Will Hate Me For Telling You This

I recently had an exchange with the owner of a vanity press (on a discussion board) who insists her company is a 'cooperative press' and she criticised me for having such a harsh view of vanity publishers. I'd basically said, "vanity presses are a complete waste of space!" She went on to say that, "the market will decide," and, "caveat emptor" (buyer beware).

Despite not liking the business she's in I agree totally with her that the market *will* decide. Which is why one of my goals is to ensure the market (I mean authors and writers) knows the real facts about their publishing options. And, that for me, means making it absolutely clear that paying someone to publish your book is vanity publishing.

Here's my problem with paid-for publishing firms (aka vanity presses), whether they call themselves collaborative, cooperative, subsidy or self-publishers (which are all just nicer sounding euphemisms for an ugly - but more descriptive - name):

- ✗ Almost all the modern vanity publishers use the same POD print company to handle printing and distribution (and for anyone thinking of self-publishing that company is *www.lightningsource.com*)

- ✓ If you were to work directly with LightningSource (which isn't their preferred business model but it is possible if you're smart enough to format a Word document and are able to create a PDF) it would cost you roughly £60 to set up your book and just over £100 to buy 10 ISBNs (you can't buy fewer than this if you want to actually have the ISBN assigned to yourself).

- ✗ Most vanity presses charge you £500+ to basically provide an ISBN (which they own), turn your rough manuscript into a barely formatted PDF (which you could do better than most of them using Word), provide a badly designed (or template-based) cover and upload it to LightningSource, who then do the rest of the work on distribution and postage. They almost certainly won't edit or proof your book for this price and if they've published and sold enough books they will get favourable setup terms from LightningSource. So their real outlay (excluding their marketing costs for finding new authors) is likely to be £15-£30. Nice mark up!

However, in their defence so far, you could say the £485 extra you paid was because you didn't want the hassle of setting up an account with LightningSource (easy), buying the ISBNs (really easy) or turning your Word file into a PDF (which is pretty much all they do) - but seriously - you could buy Word and Acrobat for less than this cost and you can use them again and again! But here's where it gets really bad...

✗ They'll typically sell books to the author at a percent discount off retail (if they're nice it could be 80% yet it's often more like 60% and less). If they do base the price on the actual production costs they'll still add a nice mark-up of £3.00 and up per book (plus many make a markup on the post and packing too). If the author had gone straight to the source (LightningSource) this would be £3.00 in *their own* pocket rather than the vanity press' coffers.

✗ Now about those Royalties... Our publishing company (which doesn't charge authors a penny and provides a full professional publishing service including design, typesetting, editing, proofing and marketing) uses the benefits of POD to give more money to the author. Our royalty begins at 20% and goes as high as 50% and we're still making plenty of income with this model. Most vanity presses - after taking money off the author up front - then typically pay just 20% (and it's fixed) for any sales made through the main retail channels and maybe 35% for the handful of direct sales from their own online store. If the author had gone straight to the source - LightningSource - all the profit from booksales (after their trade discount) would be paid directly to them.

So, if all the vanity press is doing (and for a fairly hefty profit and the lion's share - typically 45% - of ongoing sales income) is providing an ISBN, tidying a Word document up and turning it into a PDF then they're a waste of space and money! Harsh or fair? I'll let the market decide!

Self-Publishing

*"Only your best should be good enough for you.
Don't accept second rate service from yourself!"*

Debbie Jenkins, www.leanmarketing.co.uk

Self-publishing provides savvy authors with the most control, most eventual profit and the ability to keep your intellectual property and benefit from it in its various forms as you build your 'Wealthy Author Empire'.

I'd be lying if I said that I didn't think self-publishing is the best route to go for non-fiction because, in almost all cases, it is. And, if you avoid the paid-for-presses and scammers out to rip you off it can pay and pay big.

That said though, self-publishing isn't for everyone. While lots of the stuff that appears difficult from the outside (like getting an ISBN) is actually very straightforward, you're still going to struggle with distribution (even if you use LightningSource) and getting taken seriously by bookstores unless you plan to publish 50 or more titles.

Deciding to self-publish is very much like setting up a new business. For me and Debs it became just that as we sidelined our fee-paying work to publish more and more. So be under no illusion, you'll have all kinds of business problems like tax, payments, stock, staff, suppliers and more if you decide to do it.

So, if I haven't put you off yet (and if I have then I'd say your second best option is to try and get published with *www.bookshaker.com*) then it's time to look at the job of self-publishing in more detail...

Getting An ISBN For Your Book Is Really Easy

Despite what vanity publishers (and even mainstream publishers) would like you to believe, getting an ISBN (well a minimum of ten) is really very easy and inexpensive.

1. Everything you need to know (and lots that you don't) about ISBNs is available at *www.isbn-international.org*

2. An ISBN is simply a unique number used to identify your book and the publisher. It does not include the barcode which many agencies try to upsell. We'll look at getting your barcode for free next.

3. There is no legal requirement to have an ISBN but if you want your book to be available through retail outlets then an ISBN is essential.

4. You have to buy ISBNs in blocks of at least ten unique numbers, which costs just over £100 in the UK.

5. In The UK? Get ISBNs from *www.isbn.nielsenbook.co.uk*

6. In the USA? Get ISBNs from *www.isbn.org*

7. Somewhere else? Visit *www.isbn-international.org/en/agencies.html*

How To Get A Free ISBN Barcode For Your Book

When you buy your ISBNs most of the agencies will try to sell you barcode images for about $25 each. Don't pay for this because a) it's a rip off and b) you can get them for free.

1. If you're planning to print your book traditionally then get a free print-quality barcode at: *www.barcoding.com/upc* (choose 'bookland' as the symbology option) and if your printer is used to creating books they'll be able to organise this as part of the job anyway.

2. If you use LightningSource to self-publish using POD then they'll provide the barcode as part of your book cover template: *www.lightningsource.com*

3. You can include a 5-digit 'price add-on' at your discretion. This can be included easily if you use *www.lightningsource.com*

Getting Distribution For Your Self Published Book

Getting distribution (or more accurately not getting it) is the biggest problem faced by the self-published author. This problem is less severe if you use LightningSource when you're starting out (which is the main reason I recommend them) because they're a part of Ingram (who serve many outlets including Amazon, Barnes & Noble, Blackwell and Bertrams) and will distribute your book in the UK, Europe and North America. In a moment I'll list the details of the main wholesalers and distributors you need to get on side but it's worth bearing the following things in mind.

- ✓ Many will expect you to pay them an ongoing fee for representing and listing your book (so the costs can mount quickly for your first project before you've made a penny).
- ✓ Many will not take you seriously (even if you're keen to hand over your cash) unless you've published 50 or more titles.
- ✓ Having distribution does not guarantee your book will appear on a bookstore's shelves, it just means your book is available to order should they want it.

I'll discuss bricks and mortar bookshops (and why they're a real pain for anyone keen to make money from books) in more detail in Step 5 but for now you just need to know that they'll typically expect at least 55% of the profit, they'll want the option to return or destroy unsold books (while you or the publisher pay the postage) and they'll do very little to actively sell your book unless you bribe them!

Here are the main companies you need to list and stock your book but they're not likely to welcome you with open arms when they realise you've published your own book!

- ✓ Ingram Books: *www.ingrambook.com*
- ✓ Nielsen: *www.nielsenbooknet.co.uk*
- ✓ Baker & Taylor: *www.btol.com*
- ✓ Bertram Books: *www.bertrams.com*
- ✓ Gardners Books: *www.gardners.com*
- ✓ Bowker: *www.bowker.co.uk*
- ✓ Pubeasy: *www.pubeasy.com*
- ✓ Amazon: *www.amazon.co.uk* or *www.amazon.com*

Seriously, for your first book (or actually your first 49 or so books), don't worry about these guys. It makes most sense to focus where you can make an impact which is by publishing with LightningSource (and getting their Ingram distribution in with the deal) and then focusing on online sales.

Self-Publishing Doesn't Mean 'Do It Yourself' Publishing

Essentially, a self-publisher is defined as someone who registers their own ISBNs and takes the full financial risk while keeping the long-term intellectual rights and ongoing profits from their book or books. This doesn't mean, and shouldn't mean, you need to do every single job yourself. So, be realistic about your skills, the time you're willing to spend and how much getting this stuff right is worth.

I don't mean to be negative here, I'm absolutely confident that anyone can get good at design and using the software packages involved in this job. This tool might help...

The Pain or Gain Matrix: Should You Outsource This?

"Don't do it yourself if you can outsource it cheaper and better."

Debbie Jenkins, www.leanmarketing.co.uk

Although I'm introducing this tool in the publishing section it's worth revisiting whenever you're thinking of doing *anything* yourself that may be better done by somebody else. Anyway, here it is...

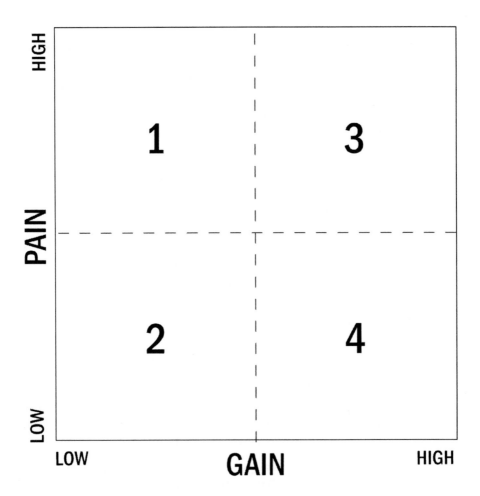

The 'Pain or Gain' matrix has two axes:

1. The vertical axis is **pain** – with high at the top and low at the bottom. High Pain means that it's either something where your skill is lacking, something that you just plain hate doing or something that's very expensive to do.

2. The horizontal axis is **gain** – with high to the right and low to the left. Gain in the context of this tool means how much money it is likely to bring in if it is done and how important it is to your overall success.

This then presents you with four quadrants:

1. **High pain - low gain (dump if you can)** Tasks that often fall into this category are usually the perfectionist jobs. Doing 10 proofs to eradicate all errors, would fit here as they will cause a lot of time and money to be spent but aren't likely to translate into enough actual cash to make it worthwhile.

2. **Low pain - low gain (dump/automate)** Some tasks, like adding the essential copyright stuff, page numbers etc. are essential despite providing very little direct monetary benefit. If they're not essential then don't do them. But if they are then see if you can simplify them or find software to automate them (page numbering is something Word Processors automate easily).

3. **High pain - high gain (outsource)** These tasks usually give you a big reward, but if you're honest, you probably dread doing them the most. Cover design and editing usually fall into this category because they require specialist skills that you either don't possess or will need to learn. Getting professionals in can actually save you money and increase the gains. I would certainly consider outsourcing the cover design (even if you pay someone to create a template you can work from in future) unless you're a trained and experienced designer.

4. **Low pain - high gain (just do it)** If a task falls into this quadrant then you know what to do. That's right! Just Do It (JFDI). Something that's easy and/or enjoyable and is also likely to bring a reward should be done – no question! I would include the writing here and (although not part of the getting published) overall marketing (as it's really not that hard and the gain will almost always be greater if you do it yourself).

Don't Go Crazy With Editing & Proofreading

Try saying no to everything for a whole week. Don't share this tip with the people you ask for favours.

Many self-publishers are criticised for doing a bad job of the edit and proof reading but the truth is that many mainstream publishers (and many bestsellers you've read and loved) will include spelling mistakes, grammatical errors and typos that were missed too.

So rule number 1: Do not obsess over eradicating every single error in your book. It's almost mathematically impossible to do this (there's simply too much interference) and the extra time, money and effort you could spend to do it will never, ever translate into enough extra sales to make it worth your while.

That said, there's no excuse for a sloppily put together book that hasn't been edited and proof-read. The simple fact is that even great writers are capable of writing stuff that makes no sense when it's read. So a good editor's job should be to make the author look as good as possible while making the content easy to read and understand for the reader.

8 Tips For Choosing & Instructing An Editor

1. Ask to see a before and after of their work. You'll learn a lot about their skills, their quirks and their tastes from doing this.

2. Ask for a fixed fee for the job based on the word count. Good editors know how many words they can typically edit in an hour. Don't pay them an hourly rate because a perfectionist editor could easily cost 2-3 times as much as an in-demand results focused editor.

3. Shortlist your top three editors and ask them to provide a sample edit of say one chapter or 1,000 words to see if they're going to annoy you by being picky or make you look good by spotting the important stuff.

4. Ask them if they can track their changes using something like Microsoft Word. If they insist on using an Apple Mac when you're using a PC then find another editor who you'll be able to easily share files with.

5. Find out what sort of edit they're doing. A structural edit will include tips on making your book flow better whereas some editors will simply do a literal grammatical edit, looking to make all the elements clearer. If your book is technical then you'll need a technical editor (this will almost certainly cost more) or you'll need to be clear that the editor is not to change anything that changes the meaning of what you said without checking.

6. Check their experience. The skills required for good non-fiction editing are very different from those you'd need to edit a fiction book. If they say they can do both then be wary and remember to get them to give you a demo.

7. Brief them and tell them what you don't want them to do as well as what you do want (refer to Style Rules – Consistency and Standards in Step 3 and use this as the basis of your brief). I've seen editors go through an entire book and add double spaces after punctuation because that's how they were taught to do it when they learned their art on typewriters. However, messing about with spacing is a job for the typeset and your typesetter will just have to go back through and remove these extra and unnecessary additions.

8. Insist that they do a digital edit. There is no longer a good reason to print out an entire book to edit it, it just kills trees, increases cost and means a delay as you wait for the bulky package to arrive in the post. Plus, if you use the track changes tool in your Word Processor you can do away with all the strange abbreviations and jargon that old-school professionals like to add to the margins.

Proof Reading

I'm not being flippant when I say this but seriously, don't devote too much time to eradicating every last error. It doesn't make financial sense and can become a costly obsession that doesn't translate to increased sales.

I typically ask the editor to fix any typos and spellings as part of their first edit and then get a proof reader (I suggest finding another person for this job as you and the editor are likely to be word blind by this point) to go over the final manuscript with a specific brief to...

☐ Spot any final spelling mistakes (don't rely on software to do this 100% right).

☐ Spot any typos (not spelling mistakes but mistyped words or the wrong words that get mixed up like 'there' and 'their').

☐ Spot any formatting goofs (multiple exclamations, quotes in the wrong place etc.)

☐ Report these errors in a separate place (like an email) identifying the paragraph, line and page with suggestions.

☐ I don't let the proof reader loose on the actual manuscript because this extra interference just increases the chances of a new rogue error finding its way in.

☐ Once this edit is done then go to the typeset stage and then do a final pre-press proof where you look for the same errors again and also look for formatting goofs (see my notes on Typesetting & Designing Your Book Interior in a few pages time).

Because the proof only requires decent spelling skills and an eye for detail you shouldn't be paying a whole lot for this (certainly not what you should pay an editor) and may be able to recruit the help of a literate friend, spouse or business partner.

Why Most Book Coaches Aren't Worth Their Fees

*"Edit your business and life.
What can you do without?"*

Joe Gregory, www.leanmarketing.co.uk

Some book coaches are great and some writers really need their help. However, too many of the book coaches I've seen aren't very good at all. They usually attempt to do the job of an agent (but charge you up front or refer you to a vanity press that pays them a finder's fee), writing coach (which is often where they're most useful), editor (even if they're not really too good at it) and proof reader (which you shouldn't have to pay so much for). My experience is that they charge you more than you'd pay the individuals involved in these professions while giving you an inferior service.

I'm not applying this to *all* book coaches but too many of the book coaches I've seen are mediocre editors or struggling authors who've decided to start their own business and charge more than a good editor would charge for an inferior job.

My advice is to find the skills individually and only use a *writing* coach if you need help with the *writing* but check their credentials first. Remember that every penny you spend at this stage is a cost and you don't make any money until your book is in print and selling. So don't over-expose yourself to financial risk by employing someone who's an unnecessary cost.

Comparison: Print On Demand Printers

Some people still don't quite get that POD (Print On Demand) is simply a print and distribution model and not the description of a particular type of publisher.

It doesn't help when some of the companies on the following list – who are essentially printers – also try to sell services more suited to vanity presses. However, for the purpose of this comparison we're assuming you're using their basic printing service and are not paying for all the extras. If you *do* pay for the extras you may as well go straight back to the list of vanity presses and choose one of those because your job will be easier and just as unprofitable.

Please note: the following comparison is independent and has been compiled based on the best available data. If you feel we've misrepresented one of these providers then contact us and we'll update the book immediately as well as post an addendum at *www.publishingacademy.com*

Your Print On Demand Self-Publishing Options At-A-Glance	LULU.COM	CREATESPACE.COM	BOOKSURGE.COM	LIGHTNINGSOURCE.COM
Let You Set Your Own Trade Discount & Terms (Good)	•			•
Force You To Provide Amazon With 60%+ Discount (Bad)		•	•	
Relatively Cheap Production Costs Per Unit			•	•
Relatively Expensive Production Costs Per Unit	•	•		
Good Discount For Larger Orders (50+)			•	•
Choice of Low Cost (Instead of Overpriced) Delivery Options	•			•
Perfect Bound Option (Paperback)	•	•	•	•
Dust Jacket Option (Hardback)	•		•	•
Case Bound Option (Hardback)	•		•	•
Coil Bound Option (Paperback)	•			
Saddle Stitch Option (Paperback)	•		•	•
Only Standard Trade Sizes Available			•	•
Special (Pocketbook/Square) Sizes Available	•	•		
Colour Printing Capability	•	•	•	•
Amazon Distribution But With Variable Availability (Included)				•
Amazon Distribution & Best Availability (Included)		•	•	
Amazon Distribution But With Variable Availability (If You Pay Extra)	•			
Wider Distribution To Offline Bookstores (Not Just Online)				•
Expect You To Publish Books Under Your Own Imprint (Good)				•
Will Mark Your Books As Published By Them (Bad)	•	•	•	
Specifically Targeting Individuals (Beginner Friendly)	•	•		
Attempting To Target Everyone (Though Not Beginner Friendly)			•	
Specifically Targeting Publishing Companies (Advanced)				•
Offer A Free Setup Option for First Time Self-Publisher	•	•		
Less Than £100 Setup for First Time Self-Publisher			•	•
Will Attempt To Sell You Expensive "Vanity Press" Style Services	•		•	
Provide/Sell ISBN (But It Belongs To Them)	•	•	•	
Expect You To Provide Your Own ISBN (Recommended Anyway)				•

Working With LightningSource.com

I'm going to make a firm recommendation here and say, if you want to make a real go of it as a self-publisher then ignore the rest and go straight to LightningSource. I don't make this recommendation lightly as I'd much rather keep them to myself (and they're busy enough as it is) but we've reviewed the competition and LightningSource still offer the best overall package. Assuming you've already got your ISBNs then...

1. Visit *www.lightningsource.com* or *www.lightningsource.co.uk*

2. Click the link to 'Setup A New Account' and then select the 'Publisher Option' – the other option will send you straight to a list of vanity presses.

3. You're entitled to choose the 'Publisher Option' because by the end of this section you'll be in a position to handle all of the self publishing elements yourself.

4. Follow all the instructions for setting up your account.

5. LightningSource has excellent and very detailed resources which, if you're doing all the design and production yourself, are easy to follow. If you're paying professionals to do the design, packaging and typeset then these resources will give them all the information they need.

If you want a really detailed guide to working with LightningSource with lots of very specific information and step-by-step instructions then I highly recommend buy Aaron Shepard's excellent, detailed and well-researched *Aiming At Amazon* and Morris Rosenthal's brilliant and easy-to-follow *Print On Demand Book Publishing*.

Software All Self-Publishers Need

I've included what I use and tips for doing this on the cheap. That said, even if some of the software companies mentioned have very customer-unfriendly policies they're largely responsible (in a good way) for where we are today so they deserve to be rewarded. So don't buy dodgy or pirated software because you'll essentially be hurting everyone!

✓ **A Word Processor.** I suggest Microsoft Word (*www.microsoft.com*) but if you're really broke, stingy or you don't like Bill Gates, then *www.openoffice.org* provides a completely free set of Microsoft Office-like tools that I've used with excellent results (as an experiment) in the past.

✓ **PDF Creation Software.** Something to create print-ready PDFs. Adobe Acrobat is now ridiculously expensive (and full of features you won't need for the purpose of publishing your book) so see if you can get an old and legitimate version of 5.5 or newer from somewhere like Ebay. What frustrates me is that it was effectively half the price in the USA than the UK but Adobe strictly enforce geographical divides so the end user just ends up feeling ripped off. I've actually played with free open source PDF creation software in the past but most printers expect you to provide a PDF that meets specific Adobe standards and I've found that stuff (like hyphens and other characters) goes missing unless I use the real deal. Go to *www.adobe.com* for more information on their software but (unless you're in the USA) then try not to compare the prices between the USA and UK as it will just make you feel bitter.

✓ **Graphics Software.** This can be expensive. I personally use an old version of Adobe Illustrator. I don't need the new features for book design and will put off paying the ridiculous upgrade costs until I have no other choice; every unnecessary cost eats into our profits from books. If you're going to buy the super-duper new version of Acrobat though then you may as well go the whole hog and buy an Adobe package that includes (as a minimum) Photoshop and Illustrator too. InDesign is great for brochures and layout but I'd still suggest you stick with Word or OpenOffice for the book's inner as the time you'll save (even if you've mastered the software) will far outweigh the slight benefits in aesthetics.

If you're not a proficient graphic designer then I'd highly recommend you pay a professional rather than investing in expensive software unless you're planning to publish loads of books. My guess is that you could probably get four or five book covers designed for the same price as buying the software. Plus you won't have to go through the learning curve (which is considerable) involved in using this specialist software.

Typesetting & Designing Your Book Interior

A fortune could be (and often is) spent here but it really doesn't have to be. If you're reasonably proficient using something like Microsoft Word then you have all the skills you need to typeset your book. The only thing you're likely to be lacking is the self-constraint and eye for detail of a trained designer. But to help you here are my golden rules...

9 Golden Rules for Professionally Typesetting Your Book

1. **Keep it simple.** Use only 2 different typefaces. I recommend a serif (with the sticky out bits) like Times New Roman or Garamond (at 11-12 point size) for the body text and a sans serif (with no sticky out bits) like Arial or Helvetica for headings.

2. **Use styles for consistency.** You'll need a legible typeface for body text and then about 3-4 more styles for the different heading levels. By setting up your styles in advance you'll easily be able to change them later (throughout the entire document) if you don't like something.

3. **Avoid leaving single words on their own line** or having a single line of text from a previous page starting on a new page. These have terms like 'Widows' and 'Orphans'.

4. **Fully Justify body text**, so there are no ragged edges.

5. **Use italics for emphasis** within text and stick with that. Don't use bold, italics and anything else you like!

6. **Right-hand pages (that is the odd page) should always have odd page numbers** – 1, 3, 5 etc. And if you want each chapter to start out facing the reader you'll need to ensure it starts on an odd page too.

7. **Look at a professional book you really like and model its layout** and typesetting.

8. **If you really aren't sure what you're doing then hire the job out** to a designer or typesetter but insist they use Word so that you can easily tweak stuff later.

9. **Within reason don't sweat the internal typeset.** If it's clean and clear and doesn't hurt your eyes to read then it's good enough. This isn't so with the cover, as you'll see shortly.

My Dirty Little Design Secret

I now use Microsoft Word and sometimes Open Office to typeset our manuscripts instead of the professional packages.

The reason this is hard to spot is because I know how to model excellence and use these simple tools to make the book look as professional as possible. Seriously, unless you're a design nut I bet you had no idea until I told you!

Coming from a graphic design business and being a Mac-head for the first half of my career I insisted we buy and use Quark Xpress for our first self-published book. Sure it has finer control over typographical stuff and better layout capabilities but it's hugely expensive and you keep having to buy add-ons to do simple stuff like automatically create a Table of Contents and bullet points and working out pagination is a serious pain.

So, after doing it the hard way for, I'd say a slightly (and mostly imperceptible) better finish which only designers and professional typographers are likely to spot, I realised I could do it 5-6 times faster, benefit from useful tools like Table of Contents creators, Tables (yet another add-on for most of the professional packages) and have the manuscript in a format my authors could also see and edit (and track changes – which is a massive benefit) using my basic Word Processor and a copy of Adobe Acrobat.

We provide Word and Open Office templates to members of our Publishing Academy to make this even easier – so be sure to pop over to *www.publishingacademy.com* to get yours.

Designing Your Book's Cover

The cover is the number one selling device you have. So never cut corners here. If you followed my advice in Step 1 then you'll already have a killer title so half the battle is already won. But you can easily screw things up by getting the design wrong.

In fact, if there's just one thing you outsource to a professional then make it the cover! I'm sure editors, indexers and proof readers will be up-in-arms about this but the truth is that the cover is the thing that sells your book. And if nobody buys your book the fact that it has zero errors and is grammatically perfect still won't put any money in your pocket!

Be careful when choosing a design professional though. I've seen some real stinkers from people who call themselves book designers but have obviously never even looked at a professional cover let alone designed one. There are some truly awful amateurs out there who think knowing how to *use* a design package and how to *design* something are the same thing. They're not!

The following golden rules will help you to brief your designer (and critically review their portfolio) or (if you have design skills yourself but have never done a book cover before) provide you with a useful plan to ensure your cover is as good as it can be.

11 Golden Rules For Creating A Winning Book Cover

1. **Keep it Simple.** Simple design is good design. The skill of a designer is working within restrictions to create something striking and fit for purpose. Just because the software package can do everything from 3D effects and bevels to drop shadows, it doesn't mean you should use it. A fussy cover shouts, "Self-Published" (even if you paid somebody) but your goal is to have a cover that wouldn't look out of place on a table full of big budget titles.

2. **See it as a Poster**. Could the book cover work well as a striking poster in a bookstore? Would it make you stop and take notice? Does it communicate the core message/promise of the book and identify who should be reading it at the same time? Could you read it from a

distance (like a road sign) or do all the elements blur together into a mush?

3. **The Title is King**. The title should stand out and be the focus of the cover. You should be able to read it easily and even if the cover is shrunk to a thumbnail size (where most stuff becomes illegible) the title should still be readable. With that in mind the title should also look beautiful. Don't leave a single word hanging on its own; break the lines and change the text size so that there's a nice horizontal balance. If your title has key words then make these stand out. 'The', '&', 'A', 'For' etc. are linking words, so consider making them smaller relative to the important benefit words in your title.

4. **Logos are for Business Cards.** I came from a traditional advertising and graphic design background and my first few covers (I'm sad to say) reflect this. They often had a clever logo or motif but, as we've already said, the title is king, so a logo is unnecessary and is a distraction you can often do without. Put the words on the page first, then think about colours and contrast and then (only if absolutely necessary) consider playing with the words or adding an image.

5. **Apply The Rule of 3.** There should be no more than 3 distinctly separate elements on your front cover. In other words, if you scrunch your eyes up, then the proximity between elements should mean you typically see the title and sub title as one lump, the author credit as another lump and any visuals (or additional stuff) as another lump. Likewise, unless you have an exceptional reason to do so (say, because your book is about rainbows) then there should be no more than 3 distinct colours on the front cover. Two that contrast strongly and one more for the spaces or highlights. Obviously if you use a photo you should consider this as one of the colours and use no more than two others. You should use no more than three typefaces on the front cover. I'd personally suggest using a maximum of two (one sans serif and one serif) and use size, colour or spacing to distinguish the elements.

6. **Leave Space.** Just because you have a whole rectangle to play with it doesn't mean you need to fill it up with stuff. Space provides the viewer with a simple way to separate the elements and make sense of the design, so use it. I typically keep the Title and sub-title close (as one element) and leave a big space between this and the author credit.

7. **Don't include 'by' with the author credit.** This is not a school project it's a professional book. Look at books by big publishers and see how many times you see *them* use 'by' on the cover. Chances are never! Now look at a pile of self-published books and you'll see they use 'by' almost without question. Stop it! Not only is the 'by' unnecessary – because it's bleeding obvious that 'Joe Gregory' isn't the title – but it also screams 'amateur' even if readers can't put their finger on why.

8. **The Rule of Contrast.** The amount of books I see with colours that simply blend into a mush so the title doesn't jump out at all astonishes me. Use colours that contrast (they're opposite each other on the colour wheels you'll remember from school) and if you're not sure if they're contrasting then turn the whole thing to greyscale. If they have a similar tonal value in black and white then they're not contrasting! By the same token don't use a spindly, weedy font for the main title. Use a bold, solid and strong typeface that demands to be read.

9. **Photos Often Look Rubbish on Non-Fiction Books.** Maybe this is a cultural thing but far more books designed in the USA tend to have photographs of gormless looking authors striking a pose on them or some generic clip-art people smiling out at you. If this is proven to sell more books in the USA then go ahead. But my view is that photographs of the author (unless they're a well-recognised TV celebrity) don't help sell books. I'm not blameless here. Some of my earlier covers have photographs on them. Usually it's because our secondary goal was to raise the profile of the author but this may be counter-intuitive because the photographs may actually harm sales. Photographs should be used only when they're adding

value to the message of the book. A book on photography should use photographs. A book of interviews with celebrities should use photographs. A travel book should use photographs. A self-help book (unless it's to do with improving your image) should probably not contain photographs. Fiction uses different rules where fine art and photographs will definitely be right, but I'm talking non-fiction here, so as a rule don't use them.

10. **Do Not Use Clip Art.** Clipart is great for school projects and internal communications. It's not okay when you're trying to be taken seriously in the real world. Those 3D red squidgy-head men that seem to be marching their way onto the covers of self-published books, websites, brochures and blogs these days are simply an evolution of the rubbish 2D blue stick-men I saw on brochures in the nineties. They may look more three dimensional but they still look crap and mark you out as an amateur! If in doubt don't include an image at all. Focus on the title, colours and text layout instead! A great website for finding inexpensive royalty free images is *www.istockphoto.com*, however there's some real rubbish on here too and choosing the right image is an art in itself (and why art directors get paid so much). So if you think my picking on the red squidgy-head men was uncalled for then take this advice: you should find someone else (a professional designer) to source your images for you.

11. **Model The Bestsellers.** This seems obvious but it's often overlooked. Big publishers spend big money on paying designers and design agencies to create covers. So model them. Try and find the commonalities that are important with good book covers. How many different fonts? (The answer is not many.) How many colours? (The answer is few.) What's most prominent? (The answer, the title, unless it's a big name fiction book where it's often the author credit.) Do they use contrast to good effect? (The answer will be yes.)

Again, there are templates and examples for you to work from available to members of our Publishing Academy, so be sure to pop over to *www.publishingacademy.com* to get yours.

Extra Stuff To Consider Adding To Your Cover

Once you've got the basics right it's sometimes a good idea to add a couple of extra elements. However, these elements should not be decorative but help to sell your book. Here are extras I often use. The cover almost always looks better without them but as our goal is to sell books (and these elements often help) the small aesthetic cost is worth the benefit.

✓ A star, banner or splash offering a freebie inside. I almost always create a free bonus and sign up form to go with our books so we can begin to build a relationship with our readers and sell them other stuff later, so it makes sense to advertise this on the front cover as a benefit. "Inside - Free Publishing Ecourse" will sell more books by adding value to the core offer.

✓ Your best endorsement by your biggest-name endorser. Keep this short and sweet (picking out the really juicy part) and include the credit of this expert endorser to further build credibility for your book and support sales.

✓ A credit for the Foreword under the author credit, especially if the person writing the foreword is a well recognised and respected name to your target market.

What About The Back of Your Book?

Some people will argue that the front cover's job is to sell the back cover and the back cover should sell the flap. I disagree. The front cover's job is to sell the book. The back cover's job is also to sell the book. If your book has a flap then it's the flap's job to sell the book. Your table of contents should sell the book. Every page of your book should sell the book. All of these elements should sell the book because you can't make a potential buyer look at your book in the order you want them to. And nobody buys a back cover, they just look at it. So, if the front cover didn't succeed then the back cover should be the convincer – but never forget – some people will go straight to the back and others will ignore the cover and start looking at the Table of Contents.

Anyway, now I've made it clear that every aspect of your book's packaging should sell the book (and nothing else) let's see what you should be doing with the back cover...

4 Back Cover Essentials

1. **Author Bio.** Keep this short and focused on why the author is uniquely qualified to write this book and what motivated them to do it. List any relevant credentials and qualifications but don't write a CV or waste space on irrelevant details. Always remember the reader is looking for, "what's in it for them" to read your book. Stuff like, "I'm a loving dad" unless the book is about "being a loving dad" is largely filler and should be dumped.

2. **Praise.** Some back covers have nothing but praise because the book designers realise how very important social proof is in selling books. However, unless the praise on your book makes it absolutely clear why someone should read your book and what they'll get then I'd back this up with a little sales blurb too. Include a photograph if there's room because it personalises the book and can help to simultaneously raise the author's profile.

3. **Bullets of Benefits.** I like to open this list up with "What you'll learn when you read this book..." This is your chance to make your big promises and paraphrase the best bits from your Table of Contents to whet the reader's appetite.

4. **The Sales Blurb.** This should say who the book is for (could be phrased as "for people who want...") , what they'll get (your big promise) and why they should make their tiny investment to buy it and read it now. Keep this short and sweet which should be easy if you've followed the other steps so far.

Setting Your Book's Cover Price & Discount

"Always know what your book is really worth to the reader. Don't charge more or less than this."

Joe Gregory, www.leanmarketing.co.uk

I was recently asked by a book coach how much she should charge her client for helping them work out the cover price of their book by doing a detailed competitor analysis. After laughing in her face I said, "You shouldn't be doing an in-depth competitive analysis at all unless you can guarantee it will make them more in future profits than it will cost them now."

In my experience it's really not worth fussing over the price and certainly not worth the expense and delay of doing a competitive analysis any more complicated than taking a look at the top 10 books you're competing with on Amazon!

Here's my quick and dirty pricing strategy:

1. Work out (or find out how much) your book costs to produce per unit (this is done for you if you use a Print On Demand company).

2. Calculate additional costs – like postage (per unit).

3. Compare your book to 10-20 competing books of a similar format (ie paperback vs paperback) and get an average price (allowing for different page counts and colour vs black and white).

4. From this average decide how much you'll charge for your own book based on desired profit, what the competition are doing and what the market is willing to pay (you can usually ask for more money for non-fiction than fiction).

5. Decide what discount you want (okay *have*) to give to retailers (bricks and mortar stores usually expect a minimum of 55%, online retailers typically accept about 35% before causing you problems).

6. Now do the following sums...

Cover Price x Discount % (ie x 0.55) – (Production Costs + Postage Costs) = Profit Per Book

7. If the Profit Per Book looks rubbish (and it almost always will if you give 55% discount or more) then you can tweak the following variables...

    a. **Discount** – (anything less than 55% will alienate you with most bookstores but we don't give more than 35% unless people order in bulk). I wouldn't drop this below 35% though as you'll experience more than your fair share of availability problems online too.

    b. **Cover Price** – This sounds mad but it's actually possible to up the cover price and discount together and increase sales and profit. People love a bargain, so if you increase the price but also increase your discount then bookstores will still be happy and are more likely to offer their customers money off which increases sales. Think of it like this. Something that costs £15 when reduced from £25 seems like a £10 saving whereas if it was just £15 it looks like a £15 cost.

    c. **Costs** – you can get these down by ordering in bulk and/or printing using offset or a big digital print run. However, I'd seriously suggest that the benefits (in terms of risk reduction and extra perks by having your books distributed for you) of POD (using LightningSource) far outweigh the profits you'll make by ordering a load of books and then trying to flog them. Save this for later when you've seen how sales have gone. Then you can make a better decision about the risks and rewards

9 Reasons Why Wealthy Self-Publishers Favour POD Over The Traditional Print-Then-Sell Model

✓ **Small Financial Risk:** Your financial risk is reduced massively by self-publishing using POD and, assuming this is your first foray into the world of publishing, that can only be a good thing.

✓ **No Stock:** You have no stock to carry, store or insure. 10,000 books take up a lot of space and aren't much fun to lump around.

✓ **Low Set Up Costs:** Print set up costs are less than £200 compared to £2,500 to £5,000 with a traditional print run.

✓ **Hands Free:** You only need to order books when you want some to sell back-of-room.

✓ **Distribution Included:** If you use LightningSource as your Print On Demand provider you get better distribution (USA and Europe) by default (included) than you'll get by having a pile of printed books.

✓ **Hassle Free:** If you stay out of the way of making sales and simply send customers to buy from Amazon etc. then you don't have to employ people or companies to pack and send books, or make loads of to the post office.

✓ **Easy To Fix:** If you really mess something up it's easy and inexpensive to update a cover (or correct an error to the inner) using Print On Demand. Whereas, depending on the severity of your goof, a traditional print run could leave you with with a massive pile of un-sellable books.

✓ **Green:** It's better for the environment. If a book is only printed when it's ordered you won't end up with loads of remainders to shift at the bargain depot or worse, destroyed by the bookshop who then expects a refund!

✓ **Just In Time:** It allows you to follow the market rather than leaving you with the burden of creating a market.

✓ **Free Postage:** You avoid paying the postage costs to the distributors because the customer essentially pays this and the book gets sent straight from the printer. Meaning more profit and fewer outgoings.

Step 5: Selling Loads of Books

"When you achieve a great victory some people will try to knock you down. Ignore them – your fans are waiting."

Debbie Jenkins, www.leanmarketing.co.uk

Selling books is unusual in that it requires quite a big push and effort up front, but once you've done the right things, it's easy to keep the sales momentum going with very little effort indeed.

This chapter has been written to help you do the high-impact stuff first and accelerate your book's success so you can focus on more advanced stuff once sales momentum has been reached.

The 7 Key Traits of Commercially Successful Authors

This list will help you to cultivate the marketing mindset you need to succeed as you attempt to raise your profile and sell more books as an author. You may not possess (or even admire) all of these traits but in our experience most, if not all, are common amongst all successful non-fiction authors. Here are the 7 main habits/activities that we have found provide the biggest bang for your book (sorry!)

- ✓ **Connected and Accessible:** Successful authors allow their audience to find them, interact with them and learn from them. How can you engage your audience with the contents of your book?

- ✓ **Generous and Complimentary:** Successful authors look after their peers and give first. Be nice to people and they'll generally be nice back. If you do decide to go against someone or something then make sure you do it in a heroic way, rather than a way that just makes you look bitter.

- ✓ **Thick-Skinned and Extroverted:** Some people hate to see others succeed. So no matter how nice you are, how good your book is and how much you know be prepared to get some negative criticism, especially as your success increases. Don't let other people's insecurities become your own.

- ✓ **Opinionated and Passionate:** Have something to say, believe in your message and be willing to back it up. Your passion should be contagious and you state your opinions with authority and certainty, while remembering it's okay to admit to mistakes once in a while.

- ✓ **Focused and Energetic:** Know what you want to achieve and focus your energies on achieving it. Book marketing is a long process and the hard work is all up front. So be prepared for a work out but don't give up, the long term rewards are worth the hard work.

- ✓ **Positive and Opportunistic:** You'll state your goals positively, believe that people will want to help you because people are generally nice and take advantage of any good opportunities to promote yourself and your book.

- ✓ **Creative and Resourceful:** Successful authors don't let minor setbacks get in the way of their success. Being resourceful means approaching challenges from different perspectives but also knowing how to get what you want in different ways. A resourceful author will find a way to make something work rather than making excuses or blaming other people for their problems.

You'll see, and may be upset to find, that being able to write isn't even in this list. I'm not saying it's fair but the truth is that success (in particular commercial success in your lifetime) is almost entirely down to the packaging and marketing of a book. So, if you're the world's greatest writer but you can't claim at least 4 of these traits then I'd suggest you make a living as a ghost writer instead.

Essential First Steps For Promoting Your Book

Do all the items on this list first and do them in order…

☐ **Write a Press Release that is newsworthy.** For more information on how to do this read Paula Gardner's book *Do Your Own PR*.

☐ **Make a list of specific media targets** (include publication/show name, contact name and email address if possible).

☐ **Post the Press Release** on your own website/blog/social media page and *www.prweb.com*

☐ **Email the Press Release** to your media list and follow up with a phone call for added effectiveness.

☐ Ask all your friends, contacts and buyers of your book to **review it at Amazon.co.uk/.com** – good reviews are really important for good sales.

☐ **Offer 5 (or more) free review copies** of your book to your contacts in return for a positive review on Amazon.co.uk and Amazon.com

☐ **Link to your book on Amazon** in your email signature.

☐ **Link to your book on Amazon** prominently (and with a thumbnail image) on your website/blog/social media profile.

☐ Include links to your book in any **email newsletters** you send to your contacts (if you use a template then make your book part of it).

☐ Offer fellow bloggers/website owners/social media friends targeting your market **free content and/or review copies** of your book.

☐ Offer fellow bloggers/website owners/social media friends targeting your market **3 books as a competition prize** for their readers if they agree to tell them about your book, review it and link to it.

Driving Amazon Sales

The first 3 items on this list are essential to a solid book marketing campaign. Do them as soon as possible.

☐ Once your book is on Amazon we strongly urge you to follow the **Amazon Hijack** steps here... *www.publishingacademy.com/amazon-hijack-plan*

☐ Once you've completed the Amazon Hijack steps **continue reviewing related books on an ongoing basis** to bring new and targeted visitors to your own book's sales page.

☐ Write Amazon reviews on every and any book about your subject being sure to include **"author of..."** in your Amazon name to drive more traffic to your book from people searching on your subject.

☐ Create Listmania lists related to your book(s) on Amazon: *www.amazon.com/listmania*

Selling Books In Bulk

Selling 100 books to 1 person or organisation is much more effective and efficient than selling 1 book to 100 people, so always look for ways you can sell your book in bulk.

☐ Create **bulk order forms** and offer **better terms** and discounts for large orders.

☐ **Promote yourself as a public speaker** to groups and organisations. Offer your time for free if they'll cover the cost of a book for each delegate. You can offer a good discount here!

☐ If you provide training then **stipulate that each delegate will require a copy of the book** and provide yours at a discount to your client.

☐ Find bookshops or organisations that could resell your book and **offer special perks** (like a personal appearance and media coverage for their store) when they buy in quantities of 10 or more.

☐ Be willing to **let organisations sponsor your book** (ie include their logo) when they commit to buying 500, 1,000 or more copies to give away or sell direct. This might be more difficult if you're published by a mainstream publisher.

Social Media & Networking

"Ask for more favours. If you had just one person do you a favour each day how would life be better?"

Joe Gregory, www.leanmarketing.co.uk

The key with all networking (online and offline) is that the more you give the more you gain. The fastest way to ruin your reputation is to run around trying to flog your book. Be generous with your advice, be enthusiastic with your praise and be prolific at making connections for others.

☐ **Setup a Facebook** profile (if you don't have one already) *www.facebook.com.*

☐ **Find Facebook groups and pages** related to your book and connect with them.

☐ **Search for potential friends** and/or use keywords related to your book to find friends that could be good connectors/prospective buyers.

☐ **Add pictures of you with your book** to your Facebook profile.

☐ **Add your cover images** to your profile pictures too.

☐ **Post information about your book on your profile** and wall with prominent links to buy the book.

☐ **Post nice comments** on the walls of people with big lists and/or a similar target to attract visitors and new friends.

☐ **Setup a Facebook group for your book** and invite people to join *www.facebook.com/groups.php*

☐ If you're going for a **big book launch** then create a **Facebook event** and start asking for helpers and prospective customers to join it now (Facebook is a useful place to manage the process from).

☐ Review and consider setting up a profile on the following sites: ***www.twitter.com*** (a great way to broadcast book-based knowledge and announce things going on), ***www.linkedin.com*** (recommended for its excellent groups), ***www.ecademy.com*** (the original online business network which is full of great clubs to join).

☐ **Build your contacts and network using Facebook, Twitter, LinkedIn** and other social networking sites. Be sure to ask people to introduce you to relevant contacts or tell other people about your book and make sure to add value by making introductions, offering encouragement, linking to their projects and sharing their links.

☐ **Find real-life networking groups** (like Toastmasters, BNI, BNE etc.) where you can network with your target market. **Always keep books handy** and either give them away to hot prospects/connectors or try to sell them to interested prospects.

☐ **Find real-life seminars and events** that will attract your target market and network like crazy or better still get billed as a speaker there!

☐ **Create a short (90 seconds max) video presentation about your book**, including the benefits, why people will want it and shots of you holding it. Do a professional looking book trailer using simple photographs for free at *www.animoto.com*

☐ **Upload your video** to *www.youtube.com*, share it on your Facebook page and generally share it wherever you can including using the 'embed video' tool on your *www.youtube.com* video to post it to your own blog or website. You can also post to *www.vimeo.com* too.

Building Your Media Profile & Authority

"No publicity is bad publicity."

Debbie Jenkins, www.leanmarketing.co.uk

These steps will not only help you sell more books but give you ways to use your privileged status as an author to generate more business for yourself.

- ☐ If you haven't got a blog for your business and/or book then get one asap. You can **get a free hosted site at www.wordpress.com** to get things started or download the software to host your own at *www.wordpress.org*

- ☐ **Write at least 3 book-related 'how to' articles.** Upload them to *www.ezinearticles.com* and add them to your own website/blog/facebook page and link to them in your related LinkedIn groups.

- ☐ **Look for PR angles in the mainstream news** and comment on them or make a controversial statement about them in a short press release, blog and/or video. Send this to your press list and include it on your sites.

- ☐ **Promote yourself as a speaker:** either offer your service free in return for a chance to promote your book and sell it back-of-room, or go for fee-paying gigs and increase your fees while still asking if you can sell books back-of-room.

- ☐ **Write useful, relevant and incisive posts** on your own website, blog or social network and also include it in relevant groups on LinkedIn, Ecademy and Facebook etc.

- ☐ If your book isn't already endorsed by someone well-known, famous and/or respected by your readers then keep looking and approaching because **a hot endorsement can massively boost sales**. If you use POD then you could even update your book to include it.

- ☐ Offer to **write a column** (free or paid for) for your local newspaper, a magazine that targets your readers or targeted blogs and be sure you're allowed to mention your book in return (especially if you write for free).

☐ Continuously **look for endorsements and reviews** from people that your prospective readers know and trust. Praise, word of mouth and social proof are the essential ingredients of a successful book promotion campaign.

☐ **Post clippings and links of your media successes** (stories used) on your blog/website and social media profile.

☐ **Give free books to prospective clients** to create a great first impression and to let them know you have AUTHOR-ity.

☐ **Whenever anyone gives you positive feedback on** your book ask them to put it on Amazon (preferably .co.uk *and* .com) too.

☐ Offer to **do and promote a book signing at your local bookstore** but make sure they'll be willing to take stock of your book in advance on a firm-sale-only (ie no returns) basis.

☐ **Keep writing articles, blogs, forum posts** etc (with clear links to your book) and share them on relevant sites. This will create more kudos and more incoming links for your book over time.

☐ **Write forewords and praise** for other people's books (with a credit that mentions your own book).

☐ Always be on the look-out for **opportunities to look good and sell books direct** (book signings, speaking events, local business groups etc.) and offer this service on your website, social profile and blog.

☐ Find and **post to other people's newsgroups, forums and blogs** etc. that deal with your book or attract your target readers.

☐ **Run workshops based on your book** (paid for or free) and sell your books (and services) direct to delegates at the back of the room!

☐ **Promote yourself as a speaker** and sell books at the back of the room without the hassle of organising the event yourself!

The 7 Habits of Highly Successful Book Marketers

Although you could do *everything* to promote your book it pays to focus on the stuff that really pays off. You don't want to be a jack of all trades but master of none. So, if time is short or you want to be as lazy as possible, here are the top 7 things you should do consistently to promote your book.

1. **Get expert endorsements** and brag about them to anyone who will listen. Find known experts and celebrities and ask for their help – this could include fellow authors – do something nice for them first if possible.

2. **Get good critical reviews** by well connected and trusted people – bloggers (use Tehnorati to find them), Amazon buyers (give copies away to get the ball rolling), fellow authors (review their books first and then ask if they'll review yours).

3. **Have a base for your book on the web** so you can direct all incoming links to that location. Measure the impact of your connections, build a relationship with readers and create new content about your book. A blog is ideal for this and you can set up a free hosted one in 5 minutes at *www.wordpress.org* (but more on your website later).

4. **Write articles based on your book** and encourage people to share them (with a link to you) on their blogs, in their ezines, on their websites and in their publications.

5. **Look for ways to sell lots of books at once** – speaking engagements, corporate organisations (who could sponsor your book), book clubs and be prepared to provide the best terms to these buyers. Selling 100 books to 1 person is often easier than selling 1 book to 100 people.

6. **Focus on the 'killer apps' for book sales** and feed them with new leads. Some authors prefer to keep 100% of the profit from books by selling direct but you also get 100% of the hassle, which takes your mind of promotion and profile raising activities. We prefer to send the hassle and the order to Amazon or similar online stores while focusing on raising awareness.

7. **Raise your profile by focusing on networking and publicity.** Build a good media list, take the time to chat connectors up, send them relevant and newsworthy press releases or tips that would be valuable for their audience. Offer to be interviewed by website owners, radio hosts and on TV. Offer to speak for free at events in return for a plug or table where you can sell your book. Make comments on current affairs that relate to your subject and offer your expert opinion.

The main message here is this: if you only do just *one* thing to promote your book then make sure it's to get an endorsement from a well-known, well-respected and well-connected person. Talking of which...

The Secret Of Securing Big Name Endorsements

*"Make friends with people who are cooler and more successful than you –
it compels you to raise your game."*

Joe Gregory, www.leanmarketing.co.uk

A great foreword and critical praise from people who have credibility with your audience is an essential part of the selling process. Some people will go as far as to pay for this (though I don't recommend it) because the right endorsement and association can mean the difference between mediocre and massive success.

Here's what Simon Hazeldine (*www.simonhazeldine.com*) a master of getting great forewords and the author of four books with us, has to say...

> I was recently asked "How on earth did you get someone like Dr. Joe Vitale to write the foreword for your book *Bare Knuckle Selling?*" For those of you who haven't come across Joe Vitale yet, he is widely regarded as one of the top five authorities in the world on marketing and is the author and co-author of so many best-selling books that I wouldn't know where to start!
>
> If the person asking the question was expecting an insightful explanation into my carefully considered and implemented strategy he was about to be disappointed. "Erm... I just *asked* him - and he said *yes!*"
>
> In truth that was all I did. I sent Dr Joe a copy of my manuscript, explained the benefits to him of writing the foreword (some additional exposure) and *asked* him if he would write it. I *asked* him... and he said yes! I'll repeat that - I *asked* him... and he said yes!
>
> Hmm... could this strategy work again? When I had finished writing my second book *Bare Knuckle Negotiating* I thought about who I would like to write the foreword. As a big fan of the BBC television programme 'Dragon's Den' I thought that getting one of the Dragons to write the foreword would be perfect. So flushed with my success with Dr Joe Vitale I decided to go dragon hunting!
>
> I researched the various Dragons and decided that the gritty Duncan Bannatyne (who according to the Sunday Times rich list was the 398th richest man in the UK with a personal fortune of £168 million) would be the best fit with my no-nonsense bare knuckle approach. So how do you get someone who is worth £168 million to write the foreword for your book? You guessed it - you *ask*.
>
> I quickly got hold of Duncan's PA, Kim, and *asked* to speak to Duncan to ask if he would write the foreword to my book. I didn't manage to speak to Duncan but via

Kim he asked to see a copy of *Bare Knuckle Selling* and the manuscript of *Bare Knuckle Negotiating*. Yes it was that easy... or was it?

After following up a couple of weeks later I was told that Duncan was very busy and would consider writing the foreword if he found the time. A few weeks passed and I still hadn't heard anything and we needed to go to print. I followed up again.

Unfortunately Duncan *hadn't* found the time and was unlikely to, and I was told it was a no go. After the initial batch of *Bare Knuckle Negotiating* was printed I decided to have another go. I sent a copy to Duncan and *asked* him if he would re-consider writing the foreword if I sent a draft of some ideas he could adapt. Within a few days the reply came back - *yes*! - along with a copy of the foreword for inclusion in the book. I had bagged my dragon!

You can now see the strategy... I asked him and he said no. I altered my approach and *asked* again and he said *yes*! I asked one of the richest and most successful businessmen in the country to write the foreword for my book... and he said *yes*!

We have all heard the expression "If you don't *ask* you don't get" and the biblical quotation "*ask* and ye shall receive". This strategy (if something so simple could be called a strategy) is simply to *ask*. Ask, *ask*, *ask*. *Ask* for the order, *ask* for the help, *ask* for the support, *ask* for the money, *ask* for the date, *ask* for the appointment. *Ask*, *ask*, *ask*, *ask*, *ask*. It is that simple. *Ask* and you will receive. You might have to *ask* a few times, and in different ways, but the secret is to *ask*.

Simon has since secured an endorsement from Michael Dell for his third Bare Knuckle book, *Bare Knuckle Customer Service* and high praise from Brian Tracy for *The Inner Winner*. A man who practices what he preaches!

3 Reasons Why Bricks & Mortar Bookstores Aren't Worth It

If you use LightningSource, as we suggest, then your books will be listed with Ingram meaning that most of the big name bricks and mortar bookshops (as well as many smaller ones) can see and order your book easily. However, if you go into your local Borders you probably won't see your books on their shelves without a bit of persuasion.

Some authors think that unless their book is on the bookshelves in these stores then they're not going to sell any books but that's simply not the case.

I'll show you why my own publishing company has pretty much turned its back on the traditional book stores in favour of a more reader-centric and low-risk online approach using Amazon and Barnes & Noble.

If you don't like what I'm saying then be my guest; play with the bookstores, but don't come crying to me when you realise that it really wasn't worth the extra hassle and cost!

Here are 3 good reasons why you should leave bricks and mortar stores to crumble:

- ✗ Traditional bookstores expect a minimum of 55% discount on a sale or return/destroy basis, with 90+ day payment terms – just to put a book on their shelves. This figure and terms are even worse for supermarkets and WHSmith. If we focused on these stores, in order to be profitable we'd have to pay our authors 7-8% royalties like other publishers instead of our generous 20-40%.

- ✗ Many bookshops have no centralised ordering process. One store, when we pushed hard with them for a couple of our author's books for example, said they make decisions on everything that they consider long tail – everything except for the next John Grisham, JK Rowling etc. – at local branch level, so we'd have to sell to each store individually. Well we'd prefer to use our effort to create demand with target readers instead.

✘ When you do agree to a bricks and mortar store's terms you will have to pay (a lot) to get any decent in-store positioning (beyond having your spine on show amongst loads of others) to make sales worthwhile. *The Times* reported on this practice where some retailers were charging as much as £50,000 to put books on their 'recommended programme' back in 2006.

5 Reasons Why Self-Publishers Should Focus On Selling Through Online Bookstores Instead

"Every action has a cost. Which actions steal your time and money without paying back?"

Debbie Jenkins, www.leanmarketing.co.uk

✓ Most online shops will accept 35% (25% is possible but you end up having availability issues) on a firm sale basis. Basically, once they order stock in, you get paid and it's up to them to sell the stock. This massively reduces your exposure to risk. You don't have thousands of books out in bookstores speculating that the shops will sell them (paper profit), that could be returned at any moment, in usually poor, unsellable, condition.

✓ If you stick with online sales using LightningSource then you don't ever have to handle the books (which will involve extra cost to post and pack) as it all gets done via the distributor/wholesalers. This typically increases profit by about £1.00-£1.50 per book and means no need to store/insure stock.

✓ Most importantly, as a pro-active marketer, Amazon allows you to ethically hack the system (read our book *The Amazon Bestseller Plan* for more on this) to increase the numbers of people buying your book, reach the top of bestseller lists, improve visibility, make the book more desirable and to steal traffic from the bestselling books by celebs and big budget publishers.

✓ Online bookshops also have a search engine that means you'll come up when people are specifically looking for *'your keywords'* as opposed to hoping they'll see the spine of your book on an overcrowded shelf shared with *anything* to do with 'your category'.

✓ Bricks and mortar bookstores are losing market share all the time as online becomes the new place to buy books. This trend will continue and we anticipate that bookstores (the way we're used to them) will be all but gone (like record stores) within the next 10 years, with perhaps airport branches stocking only a few of the most wide-appeal (or highest paid for) books. Exact statistics on the state of the retail market will be posted as we have them at *www.publishingacademy.com*

So in summary, I recommend that you focus your marketing effort where the customer is easy to find, where they're looking for your book, where you don't have to pay to be seen and where you can keep the most profit.

One extra blow to the bricks and mortar bookstore is the Espresso Book Machine. We envisaged a few years ago that eventually all books would be held in a central location and be available to print *on demand* at shopping malls, universities, libraries, schools, supermarkets, airports and, in fact, anywhere there's a book-buying public. You walk up to the machine, select your book, wait 5 minutes and walk away with your own individually printed edition. By working with LightningSource and their partner OnDemandBooks that futuristic vision of 'Book Vending Machines' is available today.

All our titles are currently available to buy from Espresso Book Machines around the world including the USA, Canada, Australia, UK and Egypt, and they're only just (as I write this) getting started.

44 High Impact Book Marketing Tactics That Work

"Focus on doing 1 or 2 things exceptionally well. Ignore the rest; it doesn't matter."

Joe Gregory, www.leanmarketing.co.uk

Here is a huge list of useful tactics you can include in a book marketing action plan. You don't have to do all of these things but it's worth reviewing them to see what suits your style and what brings the best results for you as you refine your plan. This list includes loads of tactics and a brief description.

Networking With Purpose

1. Use **OPN (Other People's Networks)** – you don't have to run networking events yourself just look for events, clubs and groups where your target market hang out and join them. Don't sell direct here simply make connections, mention your book and be willing to give free copies to the hosts/movers and shakers.

2. **Get Online** – *www.facebook.com* (especially groups related to your book), *www.twitter.com* (follow other people who mingle with your audience and send them useful stuff), *www.technorati.com* (find bloggers and give them mentions and ask them if you can help by providing a guest article or review copy of your book), *www.linkedin.com* (again, the groups and clubs are a great source of targeted leads, make posts, share articles and make connections).

3. **Become the expert voice** on forums for your topic – there are great forums all over the place where people ask questions and nice, knowledgeable people like you answer them. The more high quality answers you provide (with a byline that mentions you're the author of your book) the more mentions, links and people you'll get who know about you and your name.

4. **Provide constructive comments on blogs** for your subject area. Not only will you be helping a blogger who could become a useful ally but most blogs enable you to

include a link (say to your website or book sales page) with your reply. So every time you do this you'll be creating more links and more prospective traffic back to your book. Bear in mind that simply trolling other people's blogs by offering glib replies will do you more harm than good so only comment when you have something to say that will help the blogger and make you look genuinely clever and nice.

5. **Become affiliate friendly** – if you're going to sell books direct then offer some of the profit to affiliates, this may help you to gain more incoming links from bloggers. Even if you follow my advice and direct prospective customers to bookstores like Amazon you can still remind people how they can get paid by Amazon for their links. Write them a step-by-step guide or do a video on how to become an Amazon associate and earn from making a referral.

6. **Chat up other authors.** Don't view other authors as competitors, even if you have a similar topic for a similar audience. As I've already said, if you did your work to find hungry fanatics then it's likely they'll want to buy both books. So help a fellow author out and tell your readers to buy their book too. Provide them with a surprise testimonial and befriend them. You can then pool your contacts, know-how and audience to improve the success for all of you. Of course, some authors may still see you as competitive but if you approach them by doing something really nice – like publicly saying you like their book – the law of reciprocity will greatly increase your chances of winning a new ally. Plus, you can always recommend they read this book!

7. **Tell clients about your book** by sending them a copy as a gift. They're likely to brag to their contacts that they're employing the services of a published author and, if you were to follow your gift up with a request for their support you can gain a new glowing review to add to your marketing collateral.

8. **Tell prospective clients about your book** with a press release, personal note or by offering them (say the first 10 to respond) a free review copy of your new book. Some prospects, who so far haven't committed, may now decide to work with you because they're excited and impressed at the opportunity to employ a published author. Others are still likely to talk about you and/or buy your book as a low-risk way to sample what you know before committing to a bigger project.

Giving Referrals

9. **Write forewords** in other people's books. Always be on the lookout to lend a hand to other up-and-coming authors in your field by offering to write them a foreword. The more successful your own book is the more they'll gain and likewise as their book does better and better your name will be in front of even more prospective readers. If you think it's a bit cheap to go asking if you can write a foreword then simply make it clear on your site that, "many authors have asked me to review their new books and write a foreword, I don't do this for everyone but if you think your book would appeal to me and my contacts then get in touch..." Alternatively join the network at *www.publishingacademy.com* and befriend fellow authors there. We'll encourage them to pitch for a foreword with the other members so you can then reply and offer to help.

10. **Write testimonials** for other people. This doesn't have to be limited to just authors, say nice things publicly about bloggers, business people, speakers, customers and email this to them for use in their marketing. Be sure to include your name and the fact you're the author of a book (and include your website address) when you do this. You get a double-whammy effect from doing this in that you improve that person's opinion of you and, if your endorsement is considered and sincere enough, you'll gain another mention and a link back to your book where it counts.

11. **'Big up' other authors in your book.** Mention what they've said or something you particularly like from one of their books, include them in your bibliography, include them in a recommended reading list or simply acknowledge their influence on you in your acknowledgements message. Then, tell them you did it and maybe even send them a copy of the book with their bit highlighted! Don't wait for them find it and thank you, tell them straight away and you'll experience the power of reciprocation at work.

12. **Review other author's books on Amazon.** I'd generally only review books you like or can say positive things about (because you're likely to invoke the wrath of an author you bad-mouth otherwise) and then tell them you've done it. They're likely to want to return the favour (if they're nice) or at the very least will view you positively and be more open to supporting you if you ever need a favour in the future.

13. **Link to other websites, blogs and books** from your own website. The best way to gain traffic back is to be generous in sharing traffic with the people you like first. If they're hot on internet marketing then they'll see you've sent them traffic but why not just pop them a little note to let them know you've linked to them? They'll almost certainly want to reciprocate.

Giving Something For Free

14. **Free book giveaway.** Offer bloggers, magazine editors, newpaper editors, radio shows etc. free copies of your book to give away as a competition prize. If they like the idea your book will get a mention (and possibly a positive review) which will improve your visibility. Make the competition something that expires though otherwise people will wait to see if they won before parting with cash!

15. **How To articles**. Write loads of How To articles and put them on your blog and make it easy and obvious to share. Most blog software enables you to include special links to make it easy for people to share your content. I also

recommend posting your articles on your various social networks and *www.ezinearticles.com*

16. **Free items when they buy.** On the front cover or as part of your marketing offer a free special report, audio, e-course or other incentive to buy the book. Include the link to an email sign up page in the back of your book and you'll build a list of readers for your next book too.

17. **Free chapter.** Give away your best chapter. Don't keep it to yourself thinking you should save it for paying customers. They'll assume that the rest of your book is just as good so use the best bits.

18. **Give Free books to influential people.** Bloggers, reviewers, celebrities, other authors and anyone with access to people you want to reach should get a free copy. Send a book as a thank you gift or ask them first if they'll review it.

19. **Do Free Talks or workshops.** You can then sell books to your audience and gain loads of new fans for a single effort.

Writing

20. **Write articles for other publications, blogs, books and websites.** Always look for opportunities to write about the topic of your book. You may get paid in some cases but that's not the point. Raise your media profile, demonstrate your knowledge and gain new fans. Write your book as though it's a series of articles and you'll have loads of material to share piecemeal with your audience.

21. **Write a special report** and use it to build a list that you can then encourage to buy your main book and other business offers over time. This is called 2-step marketing and is often more effective than going straight for the sale with an advert or PR piece.

22. **Contribute to other books.** Writing a chapter for another author's book is a great and easy way to get your name in print again. You'll benefit from the association with them, their connections and other fellow contributors.

23. **Use Article submission sites.** There are loads of these around but the one that's given us the best results over the years is *www.ezinearticles.com* so focus on that one.

24. **Write a blog.** This can be a repository of all your thoughts and will improve your exposure for searches using keywords related to your book. Include the ability for people to comment and share and you can demonstrate even more value for the long term.

Public Speaking

25. **A book launch**. Only do this if someone else is willing to pay to host it (or unless you just like parties and don't mind paying). But remember, unless you're famous you're unlikely to draw a big crowd of media luvvies.

26. **Book signings.** The reality, even for many celebrities is an indifferent audience, poor marketing by the bookshops and confusion (with your spot by the toilet causing people to think they have to pay to use it) on the day. However, it's often a good way to get an otherwise indifferent bookstore to talk to you. Plan to do your own PR and promotion though and get some big posters made.

27. **Speeches around the theme of the book.** Create a list of subjects you can talk on and get yourself out there as a speaker. There will be loads of potential groups and you'll even be able to charge if you're good (and popular) enough.

28. **Lectures.** Students, while more inclined to steal or borrow a book (sorry I know it's a cheap shot to pick on poor students), will sometimes buy a book too but more importantly they'll talk (blog, tweet, text etc.) about the lovely author who told them some really useful stuff and they could become a life-long fan. Many students, when they finally escape university will eventually get a real job so it's worth chatting them up when they're young.

29. **Universities.** If you can befriend a lecturer or head of department and your book is good enough you may be able to get it on their recommended reading list. You could even offer their students a special discount.

30. **Video.** If you do talks then record them and put them online on YouTube, your blog and anywhere else. It all builds credibility and traffic for your book so recycle your time and expertise.

31. **Online public speaking.** YouTube, BlogTalkRadio or Podcasts, there are loads of opportunities to become a star of your own TV or radio channel. You can do live or recorded broadcasts and paid for or free events to an audience of thousands.

Public Relations & Publicity

32. **Full PR plan.** Include local, national, radio, TV and online sources. Don't go for generic coverage but pick your subjects, magazines and shows carefully for maximum benefit to your audience.

33. **Radio.** Find shows with a talking slot (or shows that interview authors) and get in touch with the producer or lead researcher to see how you can help. The fastest way to start a relationship here is to give them a call and follow up with an email. You should have a list of headlines/hooks that you know will appeal to their listeners as well as an idea of the exact slot you'd fit.

34. **TV.** Always be on the lookout for shows where you could feature. The production companies behind most popular shows can be found quite easily online and they'll usually post requests for experts, contestants and people to feature. This could lead onto bigger things and will massively increase your profile. Though I'd strongly suggest you get media training before going for this, talk to Jeremy Nicholas and Alan Stevens, authors of *MediaMasters* for tips and training.

35. **Stunts.** What kind of publicity stunts can you do to promote your book and get news coverage? Richard Wiseman (author of *The Luck Factor*) does live experiments and puts out a press call for volunteers, which is newsworthy. He then follows up with the results, so gets two lots of exposure for one effort.

36. **Statistics.** Use polls on your blog to come up with newsworthy statistics or ask your customers and contacts to share their thoughts. This provides you with a quotable sound bite and can lead to lots of coverage.

37. **Press pack.** Have your basics ready to send at any time including photographs and cover images at various resolutions, a short bio, a longer bio, key facts about you and your book, subjects you can talk or do interviews on.

The Internet

38. **Blog.** Get a hosted site from *www.wordpress.org* for free or spend a bit of money to gain more control and include more features by hosting your own wordpress site. There is no longer any reason to pay lots of money to a designer to get a web presence for your book. I recommend reading *Pro Blogger* by Darren Rowse for more on this.

39. **E-commerce.** Paypal buttons are very easy to set up and will enable you to take money with very little fuss. If you're planning to have a whole store then there are Open Source solutions that can integrate with Wordpress but you may require some specialist help to set this up.

40. **Mailing list.** Collect names of prospects and readers. Use a form with an autoresponder to encourage your readers to join your mailing list. This will help with future book sales and provides you with a way to upsell to your new fans. We use *www.aweber.com*, you'll have to pay a monthly fee but if you use it properly (as part of a proper backend strategy, see Step 6) it's worth it and will allow you to turn your blog posts into emails too.

41. **Press page.** Put all your press clippings, videos, photographs, press releases and essential media information in one place so journalists can find it easily.

42. **Links page/blog roll.** Use this to schmooze people you'd like to send you traffic or review your book in return. Don't wait for them to do it first.

43. **Stats.** Measure your statistics to see progress of your site in search engines. Another reason to use Wordpress is that you can get all kinds of stats to help you tweak your blog and see where your traffic is coming from. Use the Wordpress Stats plugin (*www.wordpress.org/extend/plugins/stats*) or for more details and extra features use Google analytics *www.google.com/analytics*

44. **Getting Traffic using Google Adwords.** Set up an account at *www.google.com/adwords* and use a 2-step marketing plan to gain leads and sell books. Your advert should offer a free incentive, when they click they need to provide you with their email address to get access, then you send them a really useful report or audio/video. You start building a relationship with them and then make them an offer of your book. This works really well for us on some of our books. The key with all advertising is testing and measuring. So set up Google analytics first!

Step 6: Turning One Book Into A Lifetime Income

"Your business should make your life better."

Debbie Jenkins, www.leanmarketing.co.uk

So, you're selling loads of books and your fanbase is growing. People, well some people, treat you with a new level of reverence and respect and your book is universally acclaimed. Yet, you're still not making the money you'd like to be making. You may even need to keep the day job to make ends meet. In other words you're getting the fame but you're not so sure about the fortune.

It's true that some authors write and sell so many books that they can stop their publishing journey now. If you're one of them then feel free to stop reading now. However, the reality for most is that the true money in books isn't in the books at all. And that's what this section is about. I'll share with you principles and approaches to turn the success of your book into a full-time and life-time income.

This is the place where your status as an author gets interesting and really lucrative. It's not all going to happen by itself but the groundwork has now been done to provide you with serious earning potential and to become a truly Wealthy Author.

First we'll introduce some useful principles for maximising your wealth and then we'll drill down into some specific things you can do to cash in on your book's success and multiply your income.

3 Immutable Laws of Wealthy Authors

Wealthy Authors Measure Success By Outputs Rather Than Inputs

Nobody gets wealthy by simply increasing their inputs (work). If you only ever get a single output or reward (say £5 or even £500) for a single input (like an hour of your time) then you're never going to get truly wealthy in your lifetime. Why not? Because as soon as you stop working the money stops coming in. When I talk about being wealthy I'm not talking about an arbitrary figure (you can choose whatever you like for that) I'm talking about being able to spend your time *exactly* as you wish. If you want to get this kind of wealth then you have to find ways to make a single input turn into multiple outputs.

Writing a book is a good start because it requires just one input (I know there's lots involved!) but then it can keep bringing multiple outputs (rewards by way of royalties and/or profits) indefinitely. Wealthy authors go one step further though.

They view *selling each book* as a single input and then look at ways of getting multiple outputs (rewards) from that one sale. They do this by having back-end products and services (that provide much more profit) that they can sell to the readers of their books.

Wealthy Authors Use Leverage To Increase Their Wealth

We've already said that wealthy authors are also lazy authors and one of the ways they do that is by using leverage. Here are some common forms of leverage you can use to get richer quicker.

OPT - Other People's Time. Don't be afraid to ask for help. Become a leader. Have a purpose. Recruit followers and evangelists. Do good deeds so that when you ask for help people will do it willingly. You don't have to learn everything. Pay experts to do specialist jobs. If you can't pay experts up front then be willing to share the profit you *do* make from their help. Use your network. Ask and you shall receive. Give and you shall get.

OPM – Other People's Money. Don't let lack of immediate cash prevent you from making the most of opportunities when they're here. There is free money (and its legal) if you look for it. Sell advertising space in your book to fund your self-publishing project. Or find a sponsor and give them a prominent logo on the front cover in return for their help paying for production. Get all the free money you need and invest it wisely.

OPN – Other People's Networks. If you're starting without a platform then work out how you can piggy-back someone with a big network. You can try all kinds of things from interviewing them for your book to offering to pay them if they'll tell their contacts. If you're a great writer then give people with big networks (I'm talking newspapers, magazines, blogs, ezines etc.) good and exclusive content that they'll want to share. Just ask and you'll be surprised what people are willing to do if they like what you're doing.

Your Intellectual Property. Here's another reason why I advocate self-publishing. When you own your intellectual property outright you can resell it multiple ways. Audio books, foreign language rights, film rights, TV rights, eBooks, Home Study Courses, Videos... The options are endless for recycling and reformatting your content to extract further value from it.

Wealthy Authors Know That Their Fans Hold The Real Money

I've been saying it a lot. The money in books isn't in books at all.

But do you know where it is?

It's in your fans' bank accounts. Quite literally you need to convince your fans and prospects to hand over some cash in return for a piece of your knowledge and time.

Selling them a book or getting them to read your blog is just the first step in the relationship. As they learn to like and trust you further, by reading your book, you'll be able to convince them more easily to provide money in return for the other good stuff you have to offer.

This is also known as your back-end and as you'll see when you set things up with your back-end at the front of your mind, the earning potential from a single book (even with mediocre sales) can be quite phenomenal.

The Real Secret Behind The 'Law of Attraction' & Other Superstitious New-Age Rubbish

"Hope is not a strategy. Knowing what you want and taking responsibility for your actions is."

Debbie Jenkins, www.leanmarketing.co.uk

Now let me just get one thing straight. I think the new-agey ideas of sending out 'vibrations' into The Universe (their capitals not mine) so you can be ready and in tune to accept all the good stuff back is a pile of simplistic, backward, happy-clappy cow pooh. It's an over-simplified concept designed to appeal to the human tendency for superstitious belief and the dream-world notion that you can just sit on your backside, add no value and still get whatever you want.

In fact, my least favourite book right now, *The Secret*, which dresses up anecdotal stories from 'true believers' of how their thinking, rather than any other number of variables, causes everything in their life would take things further and say that everything you've got and has happened to you up to now (good and bad) is the result of your thinking. Furthermore, you just have to really 'want things' and 'vividly imagine them' in your life and they'll 'manifest' themselves.

My response to this, and I warn you that I'm about to swear now, is, "Try telling that crap to a kid dying of aids in a third world country or to someone who's had their whole family wiped out in a natural disaster you... [Deb's note: I removed Joe's suggestion again because it really wasn't nice!] "

But I digress. The good thing is that, something big can definitely happen as a result of your thinking, actions and focus, but it's far more mundane (yet no less exciting because of it) than the snake oil sellers would have you believe. Now here's the *really* good thing. I'm going to explain how to tap into the riches of the universe (small 'u') without becoming a nutter...

How Kevin Bacon Can Help Boost Your Audience

Have you heard about the '6 degrees of separation'? It's otherwise known as the 'small world theory' or the 'Kevin Bacon Game' (Google it if you don't know why). In essence, it's the idea that we are all linked to everyone else by 6 people or less.

Here's how it works. If you know just 300 people who each also know 300 people then you now have access to a starting audience of 90,000 people... One more link (or degree of separation) and that number goes up to 2.7 million people! One more link and it gets very big indeed! Do the maths if you're into that kind of thing.

You are connected by just 5 or 6 degrees of separation to anyone in the world. Now how easy does it seem to get a great foreword? All you have to do is ask your network to find you that important, famous or interesting person you want to be connected with.

So what's more important if you want to get rich?

Selling stuff to your close connections (say bloggers, authors, reviewers and other people with their own fans who you're in direct contact with) or recruiting them as evangelists and allies who can help you tap into the loose connections (people that are more than one degree away from you)?

I'd argue that the more loose connections you have the better. Close contacts are a great place to start tapping into your network but it's likely to be 'friends of friends' who'll be able to link you up with the people you want and help you achieve the real big numbers.

So what? Well I'll get to that next but just bear with me a little longer.

It means that you don't have to directly sell your book (or the higher profit stuff we're going to look at shortly) to anyone because you can get other people to do it for you instead by using your book as currency to gain their support.

In essence if you can give your book (or anything else) as a gift to enough of the right kinds of people in your immediate network then you can start a series of events that will attract a massive rush of targeted and interested people to you, your book and (if you have one) your business.

Let's see how...

Pay It Forward

Reuben St. Clair, the teacher protagonist in the book *Pay It Forward*, starts a movement with a voluntary, extra-credit assignment:

> ### *"Think Of An Idea For World Change, And Put It Into Action"*

Trevor, a 12 year old student, thinks of an idea...

"You see, I do something real good for three people. And then when they ask how they can pay it back, I say they have to Pay It Forward. To three more people. Each. So nine people get helped. Then those people have to do twenty-seven." He turned on the calculator, punched in a few numbers. "Then it sort of spreads out, see. To eighty-one. Then two hundred forty-three. Then   seven hundred twenty-nine. Then two thousand, one hundred eighty-seven. See how big it gets?"

The maths is based on the law of exponential growth using powers of three...

- ✓ Let's say you can do three good deeds a month and ask the recipient to pay it forward to three more people.
- ✓ This time next year there will be 3 to the power of 12 deeds done in one month.
- ✓ That's 531,441 (over half a million in one month).
- ✓ What if 100 people started with 3 deeds in that first month?

Trevor also observes:

"It doesn't have to be a big thing. It can just seem that way, depending on whom you do it for."

There are 2 things we'll take from the story above and an additional one (based on what we just learned from Kevin

Bacon) that ties it all together and brings it full circle so that you get the rewards you deserve...

1. **Viral Growth** - This viral thing isn't something that was invented by Seth Godin (although his book *Unleashing The Ideavirus* is definitely worth reading) or only came about with the internet. Viral growth is behind social trends, memes and diseases too. The important thing is that if something can be passed on easily and quickly it can reach and affect a large group of people very rapidly.

2. **Small Deeds that Seem Big** - The idea that the deed only has to be perceived as big is the key to how you can do seemingly huge favours without even thinking about the payback. Now you're an author writing praise for a blog or blogger and telling your own network about them will be seen as a big favour. Sending them your book, "just because you like them and what they're doing" or as a thank you for some small thing they did for you will also be seen as a big thing. The result is that they'll want to do something in return (as humans don't like to be indebted to anyone).

3. **It's a Small World** – We are all linked to everyone else on the planet through 6 intermediaries or less so the good stuff comes back around quickly.

> *"Selfishness is under-rated. If you don't gain then why are you doing it?"*
>
> Joe Gregory, www.leanmarketing.co.uk

How Your Good Deeds Come Back:
Or How Karma Can Kick Your Butt

So let's agree that everyone is linked by 6 steps or less (this may not be exact but it's going to be close). Doing favours and encouraging the recipients to act in the same way when dealing with others means that the payback will happen from unexpected sources and more quickly than you could imagine. In fact you can reach the entire world very quickly and as you're part of that same world you get the payback too.

It really doesn't take long before the favours you give out come back ten or a hundred-fold and the more you give the more you're likely to receive.

But let's get a little bit selfish here. Suppose that when they ask if they can "Pay It Back" you say all you'd like is if they could "*Tell* It Forward".

I don't want you to be a saint and I do expect you to increase the odds that you'll be on the receiving end of the good stuff more often and with more certainty. So, accept the "Pay Back" by asking them to "Tell It Forward".

> *"Selflessness is over-rated. You can't help anyone if you don't help yourself first."*
>
> Joe Gregory, www.leanmarketing.co.uk

5 Good Deeds That Can Bring Great Rewards

Here are our favourite good deeds with a clue to how you can get the payback...

1. **Ping People.** Make lists of people who could benefit from your knowledge or the information you regularly come across. When you find something juicy then share it! You never know how much it could mean to them, even though it was a small thing for you to do! I used to do this using email (and even by calling people on the phone) but now you can do it quickly and easily using *www.twitter.com.*

2. **Give Books Away.** Bloggers, ezine owners, fellow authors, business people and people with a big network (especially one related to your book) are valuable allies. So give them a free book. You could either say you'd like them to review it if they like it or just send the book and then see what happens. Some people will do it anyway. Others you can follow up with in a few months time and ask for help.

3. **Link To Other People's Stuff.** We've been linking to people and recommending people since we started in business and the rewards are phenomenal. Almost without question, when people see you've been recommending them to your contacts they will want to

do the same for you. Try this out on *www.twitter.com* by re-tweeting somebody's update and including @theirname. They'll see you've done it and they'll almost always reciprocate with something you later write. Of course, you can do this in more places than just Twitter and you can tell them you've done it too. They'll still want to return the favour.

4. **Freebies.** If you know the figures for your back-end (we'll look at this term shortly) then it's possible to give your book away for free (and pay for delivery) and still make a huge fortune. But you don't have to go that far. Give away a free special report (as a download) that answers your target market's biggest question. Tell people they can share it and be sure you've included a link to your book in it. Then as it gets passed around, more and more people will see it and find you and your book. You can do the same with videos, audios, articles and blog posts too. The key is that it's got to be really good and something people will really want to share (because it makes them look good too).

5. **Praise.** Praise to many people, especially authors is like music to their ears. So start reviewing other people's books on your blog, stick to the ones you can genuinely say nice things about. Endorse bloggers and business people (and let them know they can use your words in their marketing) and generally (and genuinely) be nice to everyone. The result is they'll do the same, and when they do you can simply say, "Wow, thanks for saying such nice things about me – I wonder if you'd be willing to put that on your blog or recommend me to your contacts – it would really mean a lot."

You've probably already realised that all of the above can work for selling your book but what about making the big money? Let's take a look at the Product Pipeline you'll need to turn all these new contacts into cash...

The Product Pipeline (Or Money Funnel)

"Hard work will only get you so far. Work hard to set things in place so you no longer have to."

Debbie Jenkins, www.leanmarketing.co.uk

Here's how the average expert (coach/consultant) tries to make a living...

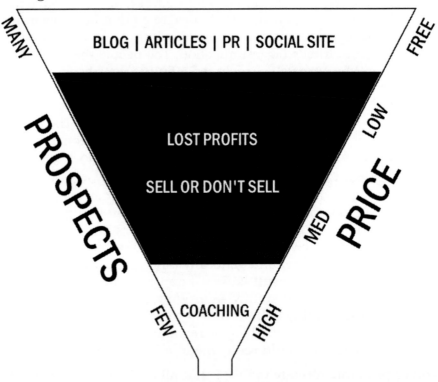

The obvious lack of anything in between what they do for free (ie marketing) and what they're attempting to charge for (typically a high cost service that requires them to swap time for money on a 1:1 ratio) means they're missing massive opportunities to generate income and operating a risky 'sell or don't sell' business model.

Here's how most authors try to make their living (and why most authors aren't *wealthy* authors)...

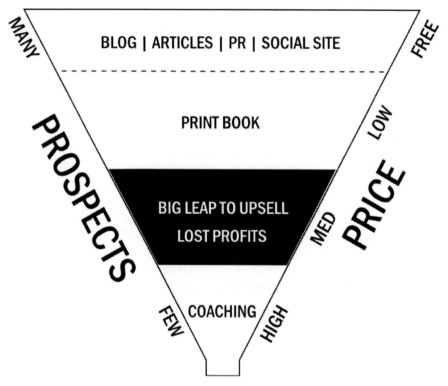

Unless you sell loads of books, write loads of books or get lucky with film rights etc. then you're likely to still need the day job to make ends meet! But as I've already said - the money isn't in the books it's in the relationship – and specifically from selling backend products and services while using your book as a low-cost but profitable lead (and fan) building tool!

Your only high value item requires you to sell your time for cash – which can only result into a 1:1 input to reward ratio. The gaping hole where medium priced products that would enable you to get paid multiple times for a single effort should be is also dangerous because prospects have to make a bigger leap from 'buying your book' to 'paying for your services' which will mean fewer conversions. It's easier if they can work their way up to your higher value stuff in easy steps.

Now, here's how a wealthy author stacks things up...

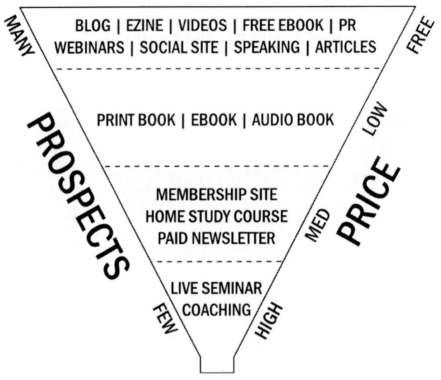

You'll notice that as your fans want more of you (including your personal time and attention) the price goes up and the number of people who are willing and able to spend money on it will go down. This means that you can maximise profit and minimise your exposure to delivering time-intensive services by valuing (and pricing) your own time very highly.

What Does Front-end & Back-end Mean Anyway?

I've tried to write this book using as little jargon as possible. In some cases I know I've failed miserably in the endeavour but it won't really matter when you come to apply what I share so I'm not worried. In the case of front-end and back-end however, I'd like to be crystal clear about what I mean. Even if you're so familiar with these words that you're offended I'm even talking about it please read the following in case your definition and my definition aren't yet aligned.

Quite simply you need to build a relationship and build a fan base in order to make real money from your expertise. As we've already seen, if you set your business and offers up correctly this will provide you with a bigger income (and higher profit) the deeper the relationship with your prospect goes.

The main thing people mis-understand when defining their front-end and back-end is exactly where the change occurs between the two. Well the simple answer is that as soon as you've made your first proper sale – and begun a business relationship – everything after that point would be considered back-end.

You could see it as a continuum.

At the start of the funnel (when the relationship is new) you'll often be able to convert more people into fans by offering something they want that's either free (like a free special report) or very low-cost (like your book). In many cases this part of the relationship actually *costs* you money or makes you very little (which is why so many authors are poor).

But as the relationship progresses, some of your new fans will want (and be willing to pay more for) more of you. At this point you may have various other back-end offers that will almost certainly increase in cost to the customer (and profit to you) while potentially taking up more of your resources to deliver.

Why A Book Is The Perfect Front-end Offer

The purpose of your front-end offer is to initiate a relationship with your target audience and attract as many people into your funnel as possible.

Many people, quite wisely, will give something away for free at the front-end (the first contact with a prospect) in order to gain permission to build a relationship with as many prospects as possible over the long term.

In Direct Marketing jargon this is called a two-step offer. You give them something for free in return for their name, address and (most importantly) permission to contact them and then try to sell them something (like your book) later.

But to call it a two-step offer is to miss the real potential of having a front-end offer in the first place. The reality is that you can include as many steps as you like and keep increasing the investment required from your new prospects as they get more and more value.

The main thing to remember with front-end is that you're aiming to attract and impress large numbers of targeted leads as cost-effectively as possible. I think a book is one of the best ways of doing this (even better than a freebie) because:

✓ A book (assuming you sell it) provides you with some profit whenever anyone buys it meaning it is a self-funding lead generator or (better still) a profit-making lead generator.

✓ A properly published book establishes your position as an expert far more powerfully than a home-made special report, newsletter, teleseminar, e-book or online video – this will lead to higher conversions for your higher-profit offers in the back-end.

✓ There are loads of well established outlets where people looking to *pay* for information by experts will go – namely bookstores (online and offline) - which an author can tap into only by having a properly published book. This provides two benefits; a larger potential audience can be reached easily (as bookstores become low paid sales channels) and you'll already be dealing with people who are happy to hand over money for something they want (you'll be surprised how many people on the web think everything should be free!)

The only real problem with using a book as your front-end offer is in collecting the details of readers so that you can sell them your back-end products and services later. For this reason I always recommend you offer a valuable and free 'reader-only bonus' inside your book so readers (even if they only borrowed your book from a friend or the library) can add themselves to your mailing list.

The Profit & Prospect Factor: Why You Can't Just Go For The Big Sale If You Want To Get Wealthy

Why am I so obsessed with ensuring you have a range of products and services you can sell to your prospects all the way through the sales funnel? What's so wrong with just going for the big money and selling the high value stuff on its own?

Here's what's wrong with it. The bulk of the money and 'hands-free profit' is in the middle of the funnel 'the sweet spot' and not at the extremities.

The following diagram overlays the potential market (which decreases) and the income from your individual back-end products (which increases). As you can see, the centre of these two variables provides massive money-making potential that only a fool would ignore:

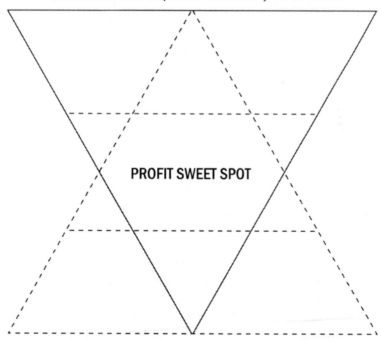

POTENTIAL MARKET (SOLID TRIANGLE) CONTRACTS

PROFIT SWEET SPOT

PRICE & PROFIT (DOTTED TRIANGLE) EXPANDS

What To Put In Your Back-end

The purpose of your back-end offer (or offers) is to make as much profit as possible by providing your new fans and contacts with something they'll love. But, as we've already seen, most authors think that once they've sold a book the job is done. This is why so many authors, unless they sell millions of books, will never become wealthy. So what *are* some good back-end offers? Well, let's take a look...

- ✓ **Book Sets:** If you've written lots of books over the years then you can package up your complete collection and sell it for a reduced one-off fee. This is essentially a high-value upsell but could make a massive difference to the profits of a prolific author.

- ✓ **Videos/Audios:** Package up all your content into new formats and sell, essentially what's in your book for 10-100 times the price. Although this seems like a cheap way to cash-in the fact is that some people will prefer to learn what you know from multi-media presentations combining video, audio and text and will expect to pay a lot more for your content in these formats.

- ✓ **Magazines/Newsletters:** If you can commit to providing regular (and timely) content over the long term then you can create solid cash-flow and lots of long term wealth (indefinitely in some cases) by offering information in this format and getting customers to subscribe for life (renewed annually, quarterly etc). You also gain a valuable (and sellable) business with ready-made cashflow with willing consumers of all your propaganda.

- ✓ **Home Study Course:** What's great about a well designed home-study course is that you can drip feed the content and allow your customers to pay month-by-month for it. Each customer will start at the beginning of the course (regardless of when they joined up) so the course content is delivered relative to when they started. This means you only have to create the content once and you can outsource and automate the delivery. E-courses delivered by email can work here but for real perceived value (and to make it harder for your content to be illegally copied and shared) you should send printed copies by post. The downside with a home-study course is that when it's over for a subscriber the cash stops coming and you need something else to sell

✓ **Memberships:** A membership website combines all the good stuff from magazines (namely lifetime potential income and a database of paying subscribers who opt-in to your propaganda) with the good stuff from home-study courses (because you can drip feed lots of pre-made content over time thus reducing the need to create quite as much 'timely' stuff). Plus, the ongoing costs to operate this are reduced because you don't need to pay for delivery and most administrative stuff can be handled automatically using the right software. Our *www.publishingacademy.com* is an example of this kind of upsell and we highly recommend it.

So far, it's useful to note that all of these things require you to perform one input (creation) for multiple outputs (payment) but, if you're willing to forfeit the time freedom of these back-end offers then there is massive profit to be made by selling your time using the following...

✓ **Seminars:** They're good because you can still get paid multiple times for one appearance. There will be a physical (space) and time (occasion) limit though to the amount of people you can reach at any one time. You can make them better by recording them and selling the recording (again and again with no limits) to your readers who couldn't make it to the live event.

✓ **Training Courses:** Again, you'll be able to sell your time one-to-many but you'll have to cut it off at some point. I'd personally suggest doing a bigger seminar (where you can reach more people and make more money) unless you're planning to make your training course exclusive, in which case, you should consider making the price for your intimate group of trainees much higher.

✓ **Mentoring/Coaching/Consulting:** If you've ignored my advice on getting multiple outputs (payments) for a single input (hour) or you simply love to work directly with people as a coach, mentor or consultant then sell your time to those who are willing to pay. But just do yourself a favour and charge what your time is really worth to you and your clients. I personally wouldn't swap my time for money for less than £1,000 per hour (it's that valuable to me) but I would expect that hour to pay my client back at least ten-fold (though when I *did* sell time the returns were often much higher than this) if they followed my advice.

Other Ways To Cash In On Your Fame

"If you're the star of your business then you don't have a business. You have a time bomb. Become dispensable."

Debbie Jenkins, www.leanmarketing.co.uk

Your increased fame, kudos and author-ity will enable you to cash in using other, less direct, ways too. Here are a few suggestions…

Increasing Your Fees As A Professional Speaker

Authors are highly sought after as speakers for companies, events, shows, clubs and other organisations. So, use your position as an author to command higher fees and to get booked more regularly.

Within just a few short months of publishing The Gorillas Want Bananas, Debs' speaking fees rocketed from £300 an hour on a good day to more than £1000 for an hour. This doesn't include the money she made on top by selling copies of the book at the back of the room.

She got so busy that we were turning event organisers away to the point where we could cherry-pick the really juicy jobs! Some professional speakers might think this is peanuts but she once got paid £1,000 for just 15 minutes and all because the event organiser had seen and enjoyed our book.

Now, nothing had really changed. Debs was an accomplished speaker before the book was published. The only real difference is that she could add the word 'author' to her speaker profile. We call this phenomenon, The AUTHOR-ity factor. When you write about what you know and get it published, you become an expert in the eyes of bookers, audiences and prospects overnight.

Doors that were previously locked quite literally swing right open for you – so start knocking and see what you can find.

Getting Paid Writing Gigs

A published author has two things going for them. First, they are accepted as a professional writer. Second, they are appreciated as a quotable expert on their subject. With these two qualifications you'll find getting paid writing jobs much easier than if you were simply another freelance journalist. Anywhere you target with your press releases could also be a good source of regular paid work.

Email or call the editors of publications where you can add real value and ask if there are any paid assignments you can help them with. You win twice. Once because you get paid and again because you increase your media profile. You may not be permitted to mention your book for paid writing assignments but many people will look you up and find your book as a result.

Becoming A Publisher

Once we realised that we were pretty good at this self-publishing lark we decided to focus on publishing other authors' work. This brings with it a load more complications but I'm confident that armed with this book you have everything you need to make the right choices to run a profitable publishing company. Some of the things you'll need to sort out...

- ✓ Choosing winning books (and authors) and knowing what (and who) to reject.
- ✓ Keeping your overheads and financial risk as low as possible (using POD, automation and outsourcing where practical).
- ✓ Sorting out ISBNs etc. – you have to buy at least 10 anyway!
- ✓ Selling books – we suggest you avoid setting up a shop of your own and signpost people to the 'killer apps' like Amazon.

- ✓ Legal stuff like contracts – talk to a lawyer here!
- ✓ Accounts stuff – getting the right systems in place from the start is really important here as you have royalties and author orders to account for as well as the various terms offered to the retailers.

I would love to go into detail here but the subject will really take up a whole book in itself and this book is called *The Wealthy Author*. Watch this space for *The Wealthy Publisher*.

Recycling Your Book To Massively Multiply Your Income

Once you've written your book just one time there are many different ways you can re-sell the exact same content. All of these approaches enable you to further build the ongoing income from your single effort. In other words you'll be able to get paid even more times for that one writing job.

If you've self-published your book then the following could be a great way to multiply your income from a single, successful book. If you're already published by a mainstream however, then check your contract, as many publishers keep the rights to your book (often with no requirement to pay the author) in all kinds of formats and languages in order to maximise their profits from your work.

Home Study Courses, Videos & Memberships

Assuming you have the rights then repackaging your content into a new format to include multimedia could be a great way to recycle the content and increase the value. We've already spoken about these kinds of things as back-end products but expect to generate a recurring income by delivering an enhanced version of your book online or to increase the value and profit by 10-100 times by creating multimedia slides, audios and videos and providing customers with a CD Home Study set.

We'll look at how this can fit into the big picture and become an automatic income multiplier at the end of this book.

Foreign Rights, Film Rights & TV Rights

In order to make any headway here you'll really need to find a good literary or rights agent who is happy to talk to you about your book. Google 'foreign rights agents' or 'literary agents' to find potential routes to getting your book published in different mediums but beware anyone who plans to charge you up front for this service.

Good rights agents will instead want a commission and/or an ongoing stake in the profits *after* they've made a deal. However, rights agents are notoriously hard to win over, so expect lots of hard work and lots of rejections if you try this without the backing of a large publisher.

If your book is non-fiction then aiming to get it published in different languages is often a good idea but don't expect agents to welcome you with open arms unless you can show impressive sales for your book. They'll assign a value to your work based on the likely sales it will make in the intended new market/medium so sales count.

Of course, everyone who writes fiction dreams of having JK Rowling-like success with movies, toys and all sorts of other merchandising but the reality is often that authors who make it in Hollywood are more often than not 'discovered' so the best thing you can do is write a great book and sell loads of copies – then if Hollywood comes knocking all the better.

Of course, in the 'do it yourself' spirit you can always approach publishers in different countries directly and negotiate your own terms and get a licence agreement drawn up by a solicitor.

Audio Books Can Get You In Front Of New Audiences

Making your book available as an audio download can significantly increase your potential market (there are plenty of people who don't enjoy reading or prefer to listen to books while on their commute). When you see your book as a lead generator for your back-end then you'll instantly realise that being found on *www.itunes.com* and *www.audible.com* is a good thing.

Not all books are right for audio though. Some print books make truly awful audio books; if your book relies on reference tables, images, charts and statistics or is a travel book that's crammed with facts and pictures then it's not going to translate to audio too well without some serious re-working. However, if your book deals with ideas, inspiration, metaphors or self-help concepts then it should be good for translation with little or no editing. In order to be ready for audio format you'll need:

✓ A good voice talent to read your book. You may be a great writer but if you're lacking the vocal charisma to make your content sound interesting then hire an actor or narrator – get them to send you a sample first!

✓ A professionally recorded version of your book. Sound engineering is too big a subject for this book but you'll want to remove any ambient noises like car noise and ensure the job is done to a professional standard – including music and intro and outro sections – or 'idents' (where you direct listeners to your website).

✓ To become a content partner for the main outlets (who provide downloadable audio) such as *www.audible.com* and *www.itunes.com* – you'll find links and information for registering with these organisations on their contact pages but here are the current ones... *www.apple.com/itunes/contentproviders* and *http://about.audible.com/contact-us*

✓ I'd start with these two above for downloadable content but there are many more potential retailers worth pursuing too (including Amazon MP3 store) so you may want to consider finding a distributor to handle all the different platforms like *www.dashgo.com* – they'll take a fee for sales but as your costs are pretty much zero you've got nothing to lose.

✓ If you haven't already recorded the audio version of your book then it's worth talking to *www.audible.com* first as I believe they can organise this for you as part of their service for content providers.

Ebooks Have (Almost) Grown Up

PDF Ebooks have been around almost as long as the internet and, originally designed to be printed or read on your computer screen, they remained the domain of direct marketers, internet marketers and information product entrepreneurs for a long time before the mainstream publishing industry caught on.

In the early days, because these books were exclusively available from a single source, it wasn't unheard of for people to be selling self-published how to information for as much as $97 a shot – even though their printing and posting costs were zero and the editorial standards far lower than you'd get with a traditionally published book.

I actually believe that the mainstream publishing industry's initial reluctance to embrace ebooks (due mostly to fears of plagiarism and the difficulty in assigning geographic rights) led to a wild west mentality amongst ebook publishers which has harmed the reputation of this medium right up until the present day.

Well, I'm glad to say, those days are almost over and ebooks have gone legit. Let's see how things are now shaping up as I write this...

For a few years now everyone has been talking about the ebook revolution and how the whole publishing industry will radically change. Each time some pundit makes a guess at the size of the ebook market they're invariably wrong, usually wildly over-estimating the uptake.

However, recent events have seen major upheavals with the 'Ebook Reader Wars' between Sony and Amazon (this will probably play out like the old Betamax vs VHS and HDDVD and BluRay contests) and the acceptance by mainstream bookstores, like Waterstones and Borders, that many customers do actually want to buy ebooks. Of course, added to this are the new mobile platforms, with Nokia and iPhone readers, which will further increase the potential market and provide clever publishers with new ways to monetise their content.

All of these advances are opening up a more professional ebook marketplace, with serious distribution options, rules and regulations. So what does this mean for you?

Well, the first step is that you need to get your book into the correct formats for the main ebook readers. If you've self-published then you'll need to sort this out yourself and if you're published by a mainstream you should ask them about ebook distribution (though bear in mind you may have signed over all rights to royalties for this format to them when you signed the contract). In case you've been asleep for the past few years, ebook readers are electronic devices that emulate a book and allow you to store hundreds of books on one book sized and weighted gadget. Once you have a device that enables you to display an ebook you can buy them, download them and read them from your ebook reader.

There's also a group called International Digital Publishing Forum (*www.idpf.org*) whose aim is to push for one ebook standard and for all ebook reader manufacturers to adhere to that standard. This is a fine idea but it currently isn't happening and it doesn't look like it will happen any time soon. Just as with other differing formats for essentially the same content though I'm sure a clear winner will emerge eventually. But, in the meantime, you will need to create your ebook in the following file formats if you expect your prospective customers to be able to read it:

- ✓ EPUB – open standard and Sony
- ✓ MOBI – Mobipocket and Amazon Kindle
- ✓ PDF – Adobe standard, widely readable
- ✓ LIT – Microsoft

Unfortunately, the process of transforming your book into these different formats involves quite a lot of hassle and hoops to jump through. Your original file will need to be re-worked for the various formats to make it acceptable to the end retailers and distributors. There are tools to help (though you'll need some technical know-how) or you can outsource the whole project. For a step-by-step guide on how to convert your book go to: *www.publishingacademy.com/ebook-conversion*-process

Once you have your book available in the various formats you will then need to get it distributed and sold. There are a number of online retailers and sites that will accept your ebooks including:

- ✓ *www.mobipocket.com* – accepts Mobipocket format ebooks which can be read on devices that use Mobipocket software.

- ✓ *www.contentreserve.com* – supplies ebooks in various formats to major retailers like Waterstones. It's difficult to get an account with them and even more difficult to get your files accepted as they have strict quality controls.

- ✓ *www.smashwords.com* – accepts a wide variety of formats and even helps you make them yourself.

- ✓ *http://dtp.amazon.com* - Amazon's digital platform for the Kindle which enables Kindle owners to buy books from anywhere, without the need for an internet account.

So, why bother with all this hassle? Well the ebook market is growing, the cost of the devices is coming down, there is more competition, the internet is more widely available and publishers are realising that this is another route to market for their books.

- ✓ Indonesia downloads the most ebooks to their mobile devices (39%), followed by US (28%) and Vietnam (9%) – source *wattpad.com*

- ✓ In May 2009 the Association of American Publishers (AAP *www.publishers.org*) reported ebook sales jumped up by 196.6 percent for the month ($11.5 million) reflecting an increase of 166.7 percent for the year

- ✓ Penguin's ebook sales in the first 3 months of 2009 are up 7 times as compared to the first 3 months of 2008.

If your book targets any of the following categories then it's worth your investment in time and energy to sell it in ebook format too:

- ✓ People living abroad because shipping books is costly.
- ✓ Travellers who want to carry multiple books with them.
- ✓ Researchers who need access to multiple books simultaneously.
- ✓ Students who need access to books immediately.
- ✓ Early adopters who like new gadgets (us!)
- ✓ Software developers, engineers and techies in general.
- ✓ People in developing countries, where access to mobile phones is high, but access to bookshops and printed material might be lower.

Your New Wealthy Mindset

The opportunities to become wealthy once you've written a book are great. The only thing you have to do is recognise them and decide to put things in place to capitalise on your book's success.

I hope this final section has inspired you to look at your role as an author with a new perspective and in the days and weeks ahead I trust you'll find many ways to cash in on your success, make your book pay and enjoy the increasing freedom you can experience as a wealthy author.

The End?

Your 30 Day Free Trial of Publishing Academy

Now we've spilled our brains on what it takes to be a wealthy author it's all up to you. The end of this book is really just the beginning of *your* journey to making your fortune as an author.

While you may not agree with *all* of our advice I can guarantee that we learned what we've shared the hard way. So try what we suggest and make up your own mind. If you've learned anything from reading this book then I hope it's to challenge the accepted wisdom of 'the herd' and use your own results and experience to determine the right thing to do.

If you want more, or are keen to share your success with other authors then you can join us at *www.publishingacademy.com*.

For details of a very special offer where you'll also get a free 30-days-pass as a Publishing Academy insider worth £15.00 go to:

www.publishingacademy.com/free-reader-trial

We look forward to seeing you and sharing more with you in the future. So keep on visiting and learning from us and our other experts and become part of *www.publishingacademy.com*.

Thanks for reading and we wish you all the success you deserve!

Joe Gregory and Debbie Jenkins

About The Authors

Debbie Jenkins and Joe Gregory are an entrepreneurial team who started their first business together back in 1997 and have been having fun making their friends and clients rich through business, books and marketing ever since.

Debbie Jenkins (according to Joe Gregory)

Debs has an incredible grasp of marketing, especially breaking complicated stuff into easy chunks, and has a knack for dragging me into new and exciting (also known as scary) projects that would otherwise make me run a mile. Her official title could be marketer, author, professional speaker, entrepreneur, publisher or 'the boss', but I just know her as my big (and slightly eccentric) sister.

She earned the nickname 'Dangerous' Debbie (as well as obscenely high speaking fees) back in the nineties due to her audacious no BS business and speaking style. She's still just as dangerous but she's not been in the limelight as much in recent years since moving to live in a cave in Spain (did I mention she was eccentric?)

Debs' background as an electronics engineer and head-hunter (the company's top fee earner in a very competitive field) gives her a unique take on business, people and systems in particular. The reason I've been able to continue working with her for almost 13 years now (some people wonder how we do it) is because she has an unbeatable work ethic and a real sense of fair play.

Plus, she seems to be a magnet for success, so it's good to stay close!

Joe Gregory (according to Debbie Jenkins)

I dragged Joe away from his high-flying career in an artsy ad agency when he was just 19 because I needed someone who was good at making stuff up (I mean marketing copy, not lies!) and thought having an in-house design and branding expert would be good for business. I was right!

With Joe's help we've battered the competition in all kinds of fields, from online marketing (we were there at the start) to consulting (we grew our business in record time) and writing (our *Gorillas Want Bananas* book was a huge commercial success) to publishing (I still don't know how we managed to publish and sell so many books in just a couple of years).

Although I dragged him away from a steady job Joe will readily admit he wasn't really suited for the arty-farty life anyway. Of course, he's the most creative person I know but that's grounded in a real desire to make everything he does translate into turning into cash for the people he helps.

Joe's not into design for design's sake, which is refreshing! If you were to ask Joe what he does for a living he'd probably say, "I make books" (which could be confused with running a betting shop in the UK) but his skills go a lot deeper than that. He's also trained extensively in Neurolinguistic Programming since the late nineties and applies what he's learned to sell more books, write faster and bring the best out of our authors, and to devastating effect too.

A Bit More About Us

After we successfully self-published and sold-out of our first book entitled, _The Gorillas Want Bananas_, we soon caught the publishing bug and decided to pack up our lucrative consultancy business and do publishing full time. So we set up publishing firm – BookShaker.com in 2003 ... and the rest, as they say, is history...

Our original claim to fame is that we managed to publish 37 books and achieve 5 best-sellers (making more than £30,000 in a single day with one book) within our first 2 years while carrying out all aspects of the business single-handedly.

We did everything, including editing, typesetting, cover design, PR, sales copy, marketing and invoicing while keeping our overheads to a minimum. The way we were able to achieve so much without the need for employees is by systemising every aspect of the business (based on our Lean Marketing philosophy – *www.leanmarketing.co.uk*), using leverage (there are great partners and multipliers in the book game) and carefully managing our time.

If you're looking for a pro-active non-fiction publisher that pays unprecedented royalties visit us at *www.bookshaker.com*

Links

Self Publishing Software & Links

www.adobe.com
http://freemind.sourceforge.net
www.imindmap.com/bookshaker
www.istockphoto.com
www.microsoft.com
www.openoffice.org
www.wordpress.com
www.wordpress.org

Promotion & Publicity

www.amazon.com/listmania
www.animoto.com
www.aweber.com/?201812
www.blogtalkradio.com
www.ecademy.com
www.ezinearticles.com
www.facebook.com

www.freeautobot.com
www.getresponse.com
www.leanmarketing.co.uk
www.linkedin.com
www.prweb.com
www.publishingacademy.com/amazon-hijack-plan
www.twitter.com
www.vimeo.com
www.youtube.com

Audio Books & Ebooks

http://about.audible.com/contact-us
www.audible.com
www.apple.com/itunes/contentproviders
www.contentreserve.com
www.dashgo.com
http://dtp.amazon.com
www.idpf.org
www.itunes.com
www.mobipocket.com
www.publishingacademy.com/ebook-conversion
www.smashwords.com

Research Tools

www.amazon.co.uk
www.amazon.com
http://books.google.com
www.google.com/adwords
www.google.com/trends
www.technorati.com

Publishing Industry

www.ipg.uk.com
www.pma-online.org
www.publishers.org
www.spannet.org

Print On Demand (POD) Printers

www.booksurge.com

www.createspace.com
www.lightningsource.com
www.lightningsource.co.uk
www.lulu.com

ISBN Agencies & Barcodes

www.isbn-international.org
www.isbn.nielsenbook.co.uk
www.isbn.org
www.isbn-international.org/en/agencies.html
www.barcoding.com/upc

Book Distributors & Wholesalers

www.ingrambook.com
www.nielsenbooknet.co.uk
www.btol.com
www.bertrams.com
www.gardners.com
www.bowker.co.uk
www.pubeasy.com

Bibliography

1001 Ways to Market Your Books, John Kremer, 091241149X
The 22 Immutable Laws of Marketing, Al Ries & Jack Trout, 1861976100
The 4-Hour Workweek, Timothy Ferris, 0091923727
Aiming At Amazon, Aaron Shepard, 093849743X
The Amazon Bestseller Plan, Debbie Jenkins & Joe Gregory, www.publishingacademy.com
The Art of Contrary Thinking, Humphrey Neill, 087004110X
Bare Knuckle Negotiating, Simon Hazeldine, 1905430140
Bare Knuckle Selling, Simon Hazeldine, 1905430051
Blocks, Tom Evans, www.publishingacademy.com
The Chicago Manual of Style, University of Chicago Press, 0226104036

Dan Poynter's Self-Publishing Manual: How to Write, Print and Sell Your Own Book, Dan Poynter, 1568601425

E-myth Revisited, Michael E Gerber, 0887307280

Get Your Book Published, Suzan St Maur

Go it Alone: The Streetwise Secrets of Self-employment, Geoff Burch, 1841124702

Google Adwords for Dummies, Howie Jacobson, 0470455772

The Gorillas Want Bananas, Joe Gregory & Debbie Jenkins, 0954568109

How to Get Rich, Felix Denis, 009192166X

Influence, Robert Cialdini, 006124189X

It's Called Work for a Reason! Your Success Is Your Own Damn Fault, Larry Winget, 159240281X

Kickstart Your Business, Robert Craven, 0753509733

MediaMasters, Alan Stevens & Jeremy Nicholas, 1905430612

The Midas Method, Stuart G Goldsmith, 1871379008

The Mindmap Book, Tony Buzan & Barry Buzan, 1406612790

The Money Gym, Nicola Cairncross, 0954568184

No B.S. Direct Marketing, Dan Kennedy, 1932531572

No B.S. Wealth Attraction for Entrepreneurs, 193253167X

Oxford Guide To Style, Robert Ritter, 0198691750

Permission Marketing, Seth Godin, 1416526668

Persuasion Skills Black Book, Rintu Basu, 190543054X

Powerwriting, Suzan St Maur, 0273659065

Print On Demand Book Publishing, Morris Rosenthal, 0972380132

ProBlogger: Blogging Your Way to a 6 Figure Income, Darren Rowse & Chris Garrett, 0470246677

Release The Book Within, Jo Parfitt, 1905430264

Selling The Invisible: A Field Guide to Modern Marketing, Harry Beckwith, 0446520942

Strategies of Genius, Volume 1, Robert Dilts, 091699032X

Trance-formations: NLP and the Structure of Hypnosis, John Grinder & Richard Bandler, 0911226230

Tribes, Seth Godin, 0749939753

Unleashing the Ideavirus, Seth Godin, 074322065X

The Well-Fed Self-Publisher, Peter Bowerman, 0967059860

The Writers' and Artists' Yearbook 2010, 1408111276

THE
Amazon
Bestseller
PLAN

HOW TO MAKE YOUR BOOK AN AMAZON BESTSELLER IN 24 HOURS OR LESS

DEBBIE JENKINS
JOE GREGORY

www.publishingacademy.com

Get Your
Book
Published

HOW TO DEVISE, WRITE & SELL YOUR NON-FICTION BOOK TO PUBLISHERS

SUZAN ST MAUR

www.publishingacademy.com

Lightning Source UK Ltd.
Milton Keynes UK
22 December 2009

147838UK00001B/39/P